GWENDOLYN MACEWEN

NOMAN

This book is dedicated to all the strangers in Kanada

HOUSE OF THE WHALE

Of course I was never a whale; I was an Eagle. This prison is a cage for the biggest bird of all. I'm waiting for them to work their justice, you see, and while I'm waiting I'm writing to you, Aaron, good friend, joker. The hours pass quickly here, strange to say; I have all kinds of diversions. The nice fat guard with the bulbous nose and the starfish wart at the tip often greets me as he makes his rounds. I make a point of waiting at the front of the cell when I know he's coming. And then there's Mario in the next cell who taps out fascinating rhythms at night with his fingernails against the walls.

I don't have an eraser with me, Aaron, so any mistakes I make will have to stay as they are, and when the pencil wears down, that will be that.

I can't help thinking how young I still am—23. Twenty-three. Can I tell you about my life again? It was normal at first. I wrenched my mother's legs apart and tore out of her belly, trailing my sweet house of flesh behind me. I lay on a whaleskin blanket and watched the water; I sucked milk; I cried. I was wrapped up in thick bearskin in winter. I was bathed in the salt water of the sea. My mother was taller than all the mountains from where I lay.

There were the Ravens and the Eagles. You already know which I was. When I was old enough to take notice of things around me, I saw the half-mile line of our houses facing the waters of Hecate Strait. And I saw the severe line of the totems behind them, guarding the village, facing the sea—some of them vertical graves for the dead chiefs of old. Some totems, even then, had fallen, but our Eagle still looked down on us from the top of the highest one, presiding over the angular boats on the beach, the rotting cedar dugouts and black poplar skiffs. (Someone ages before had suggested getting motors for them— the boats, that is—and the old men of the village almost died.)

I was turned over to my uncle's care after I passed infancy, and he spoke to me in the Skittegan tongue and told me tales in the big cedar plank house. I've long since forgotten the language, you know that, but the stories remain with me, for stories are pictures, not words. I learned about the Raven, the Bear, the Salmon-Eater and the Volcano Woman—just as your children someday will learn all about Moses or Joshua or Christ.

I never knew my father; after planting me in my mother's belly he left to go and work in the Commercial Fisheries on the mainland. He forsook the wooden hooks and cuttlefish for the Canneries—who could blame him? Secretly, I admired him and all those who left the island to seek a fortune elsewhere, to hook Fate through the gills. But he never came back.

Our members had once been in the thousands, but had dwindled to hundreds. My grandfather, who was very old, remembered the smallpox that once stripped the islands almost clean. He remembered how the chiefs of the people were made to work in the white man's industries with the other men of the tribe, regardless of their rank; he remembered how the last symbols of authority were taken away from the chiefs and *shamans*. A chief once asked the leader of the white men if he might be taken to *their* island, Eng-

6

land, to speak with the great white princess, Victoria—but he was refused.

Sometimes I heard my grandfather cursing under his breath the Canneries and hop fields and apple orchards on the mainland. I think he secretly wished that the Sacred-One-Standing-and-Moving who reclined on a copper box supporting the pillar that held the world up—would shift his position and let the whole damn mess fall down.

When I was young some of our people still carved argillite to earn extra money. It was a dying art even then, but the little slate figures always brought something on the commercial market. The Slatechuk quarry up Slatechuk creek wasn't far from Skidegate; and there was an almost inexhaustible supply of the beautiful black stone, which got shaped into the countless figures of our myths. I remember having seen Louis Collison, the last of the great carvers, when I was still a child. I watched his steady gnarled hands creating figures and animals even I didn't know about, and I used to imagine that there was another Louis Collison, a little man, who lived inside the argillite and worked it from the inside out.

(The fine line, Aaron, between what is living and what is dead ... what do I mean, exactly? That party you took me to once in that rich lady's house where everyone was admiring her latest artistic acquisition—a *genuine Haida* argillite sculpture. It illustrated the myth of Rhpisunt, the woman who slept with a bear and later on bore cubs, and became the Bear Mother. Well, there were Rhpisunt and the bear screwing away in the black slate; Rhpisunt lay on her back, legs up, straddling the beast, her head thrown back and her jaws wide open with delight—and Mrs. What's-Her-Name kept babbling on and on about the 'symbolic' meaning of the carving until I got mad and butted in and told her it was obviously a bear screwing a woman, nothing more, nothing less. She looked upset, and I was a little drunk

7

and couldn't resist adding, 'You see, I too am *genuine Haida.*' And as the party wore on I kept looking back at the elaborate mantelpiece and the cool little slate sculpture, and it was dead, Aaron, it had *died*—do you see?)

My mother wove baskets sometimes and each twist and knot in the straw was another year toward her death. And she sometimes lit the candlefish, the *oolakan* by night, and we sat around its light, the light of the sea, the light of its living flesh. Sometimes the old *shaman* would join us, with his dyed feathers and rattles, and do magic. I saw souls and spirits rising from his twisted pipe; I saw all he intended me to see, though most of the people left in the village laughed at him, secretly of course.

My grandfather was so well versed in our legends and myths that he was always the man sought out by the myth-hunters—museum researchers and writers from the mainland—to give the Haida version of such and such a tale. My last memory of him, in fact, is when he was leaning back in his chair and smoking his pipe ecstatically and telling the tale of Gunarh to the little portable tape-recorder that whirred beside him. Every researcher went away believing he alone had the authentic version of such and such a myth, straight from the Haida's mouth—but what none of them ever knew was that grandfather altered the tales with each re-telling. 'It will give them something to fight about in their books,' he said. The older he got, the more he garbled the tales, shaking with wicked laughter in his big denim overalls when the little men with tape recorders and note-books went away.

Does he think of me now, I wonder? Is he still alive, or is he lying in a little Skidegate grave after a good Christian burial—a picture of an eagle on the marble headstone as a last reminder of the totem of his people? Is he celebrating his last *potlache* before the gates of heaven, and has the *shaman* drummed his long dugout through waves of clouds? Are the ceremonial fires burning now, and is my grandfather throwing in his most precious possessions—his blue demim overalls, his pipe?

(Remember, Aaron, how amazed you were when I first told you about the *potlache*? 'Why didn't the chiefs just *exhibit* their wealth?' you argued, and I told you they felt they could prove their wealth better by demonstrating how much of it they could *destroy*. Then you laughed, and said you thought the *potlache* had to be the most perfect parody of capitalism and consumer society you'd ever heard of. 'What happened,' you asked, 'if a chief squandered everything he owned and ended up a poor man?' And I explained how there were ways of getting wealthy again—for instance, the bankrupt chief could send some sort of gift to a rival chief, knowing that the returned favour had to be greater than the original one. It was always a matter of etiquette among our people to outdo another man's generosity.)

Anyway, I lie here and imagine grandfather celebrating a heavenly *potlache*—(heaven is the only place he'll ever celebrate it, for it's long since been forbidden by the government here on earth)—and the great Christian gates are opening for him now, and behind him the charred remains of his pipe and his blue denims bear witness to the last *potlache* of all.

Some of my childhood playmates were children of the white teacher and doctor of Skidegate, and I taught them how to play *Sin*, where you shuffle marked sticks under a mat and try to guess their positions. They got sunned up in summer until their skins were as copper as mine; we sat beneath the totems and compared our histories; we sat by the boats and argued about God. I read a lot; I think I must have read every book in the Mission School. By the time I was fifteen I'd been to the mainland twice and come back with blankets, potato money and booze for the old *shaman*.

I began to long for the mainland, to see Vancouver, the

forests of Sitka spruce in the north, mountains, railroads, lumber camps where Tsimsyan and Niskae workers felled trees and smashed pulp. My uncle had nothing to say when I announced that I was going to go and work at 'the edge of the world'—but my grandfather put up a terrific fight, accusing me of wanting to desert my people for the white man's world, accusing my mother of having given birth to a feeble-spirited fool because on the day of my birth she accepted the white man's pain-killer and lay in 'the sleep like death' when I came from her loins. And then he went into a long rambling tale of a day the white doctor invited the *shaman* in to witness his magic, and the *shaman* saw how everything in the doctor's room was magic white, to ward off evil spirits from sick flesh, and he saw many knives and prongs shining like the backs of salmon and laid out in neat rows on a white sheet; from this he understood that the ceremony would not work unless the magical pattern of the instruments was perfect. Then the doctor put the sick man into the death-sleep, and the *shaman* meanwhile tried to slip the sick soul into his bone-box, but he couldn't because the doctor's magic was too powerful to be interfered with. It was only when the doctor laid out exactly four knives and four prongs onto another white sheet, that the *shaman* realized the doctor had stolen the sacred number four from us to work his magic.

I worked north in a lumber camp for a while; we were clearing a patch of forest for an airplane base. In one year I don't know how many trees I killed—too many, and I found myself whispering 'Sorry, tree' every time I felled another one. For *that* I should be in prison—wouldn't you think? Wasn't it worse to destroy all those trees than do what I did? Oh well, I can see you're laughing in your beer now, and I don't blame you. Anyway, I really wanted to tell you about Jake and the other guys in the bunkhouse, and what a great bunch they were. I learned a lot about girls and things from them, and since I didn't have any stories of my own like that to tell them, I told them the myth of Gunarh—you know the one; you said the first part of it's a lot like a Greek myth—and all the guys gathered around, and Jake's mouth was hanging open by the time I got to the part about Gunarh's wife eating nothing but the sweetbreads of male seals. . . .

'Then she took a lover,' I went on, 'and her husband discovered her infidelity and made a plan.'

'Yea, yea, go on, he made a *plan*!' gasped Jake.

'He—'

'SHADDUP, YOU GUYS, I'M TRYING TO LISTEN!'

'When they were asleep after a hard night, the lover and the wife. . . .'

'Hear that, guys—a HARD night!'

'Jake, will ya SHADDUP!'

'—Gunarh came in and discovered them together. He killed the lover and cut off his head and his—'

'Jesus CHRIST!'

'Jake, will ya SHADDUP!!'

'—and put them on the table . . . .'

'Put *what* on the table?'

'It ain't the *head* boys!'

'Jesus CHRIST!'

'So the next morning his wife found her lover gone, and she went to the table for breakfast—you remember what she usually ate—and instead of . . . .'

'O no! I'm sick, you guys, I'm sick!'

'SHADDUP!'

'—well, she ate *them* instead.'

'Jake, will ya lie down if you can't take it?'

I never did finish the story, because they went on and on all night about what Gunarh's wife ate for breakfast, and Jake kept waking up and swearing he was never going to listen to one of my stories again, because it was for sure all Indians had pretty dirty minds to think up things like that.

Almost before I knew it, my year was up and I was on a train heading for Vancouver; the raw gash I had made in the forest fell back behind me.

At first I spent a week in Vancouver watching the people carry the city back and forth in little paper bags; I stayed in a strange room with a shape like a big creamy whale in the cracked plaster on the ceiling, and curtains coloured a kind of boxcar red that hung limply and never moved. I drank a lot and had some women and spent more money than I intended, and after standing three mornings in a row in a line-up in the Unemployment Office, I bumped into you, Aaron, remember, and that was the beginning of our friendship. You had a funny way of looking at a person a little off-centre, so I was always shuffling to the left to place myself in your line of focus. I can't remember exactly what we first talked about; all I know is, within an hour we'd decided to hitch-hike to Toronto, and that was that. At first I hesitated, until you turned to me staring intently at my left ear and said, 'Lucas George, you don't want to go back to Skidegate, you're coming east.' And it was that careless insight of yours that threw me. You always knew me well, my friend. You knew a lot, in fact—and sometimes I was sure you kept about 50% of your brain hidden because it complicated your life. You were always a little ahead of yourself—was that the reason for your nervousness, your impatience? You could always tell me what I was thinking, too. You told me I was naive and you liked me for that. You predicted horrible things for me, and you were right. You said my only destiny was to lose myself, to become neither Indian nor white but a kind of grey nothing, floating between two worlds. Your voice was always sad when you spoke like that. . . .

Hey Aaron, do you still go through doors so quickly that no one remembers seeing you open them first?

My grandfather's tales, if he's still alive, are growing taller in Skidegate. My mother's baskets, if she's still alive, are getting more and more complicated—and the salmon are skinnier every season. My time's running out, and I'd better finish this letter fast.

You were silent in BC but you talked all the way through Alberta and Saskatchewan; we slept through Manitoba and woke up in Ontario. The shadows of the totems followed me, growing longer as the day of my life grew longer. The yellow miles we covered were nothing, and time was even less.

'Lucas,' you turned to me, 'I forgot to tell you something. In BC you were still something. Here, you won't even exist. You'll live on the sweet circumference of things, looking into the centre; you'll be less than a shadow or a ghost. Thought you'd like to know.'

'Thanks for nothing,' I said. 'Anyway, how do *you* know?'

'I live there too, on the circumference,' you said.

'What do you do, exactly?'

'I'm an intellectual bum,' you answered, 'I do manual work to keep my body alive. Sometimes I work above the city, sometimes I work below the city, depending on the weather. Skyscrapers, ditches, subways, you name it, I'm there....'

Aaron, I only have a minute left before they turn the lights out for the night. I wanted to ask you....

too late   out
          they're

'Well,' you said, the first day we were in the city, 'Welcome to the House of the Whale, Lucas George.'

'What do you mean?' I said.

'Didn't you tell me about Gunarh and how he went to the bottom of the sea to rescue his wife, who was in the House of the Whale.'

'Yes, but—'

'Well I'm telling you *this* is the House of the Whale, this city, this place. Ask me no questions, and I'll tell you no lies. This, this is where you'll find your *psyche*.'

'My *what*?'

'This is where you'll find what you're looking for.'

'But, Aaron, I'm not looking for anything really!'

'Oh yes you are. . . .'

We stood looking at City Hall with its great curving mothering arms protecting a small concrete bubble between them. Behind us was Bay Street and I turned and let my eyes roll down the narrow canyon toward the lake. 'That's the Wall Street of Toronto,' you said. 'Street of Money, Street of Walls. Don't worry about it; you'll never work there.'

'So what's down there?' I asked, and you pointed a finger down the Street of Walls and said, 'That's where the whales live, Lucas George. You know all about them, the submerged giants, the supernatural ones. . . .'

'The whales in our stories were gods,' I protested. And you laughed.

'I wish I could tell you that this city was just another myth, but it's not. It smacks too much of reality.'

'Well, *what else*!' I cried, exasperated with you. First it's a whale house, then you want it to be a myth—couldn't it just be a city, for heaven's sake?'

'Precisely. That's precisely what it is. Let's have coffee.'

We walked past City Hall and I asked you what the little concrete bubble was for.

'Why, that's the egg, the seed,' you said.

'Of *what*?'

'Why, Lucas George, I'm surprised at you! Of the *whale*, of course! Come on!'

'Looks like a clam shell to me,' I said. 'Did I ever explain to you where mankind came from, Aaron? A clam shell, half-open, with all the little faces peering out. . . .'

'I'll buy that,' you said. 'It's a clam shell. Come on!'

I got a job in construction, working on the high beams of a bank that was going up downtown. 'Heights don't bother you Indians at all, do they?'the foreman asked me. 'No,' I said. 'We like tall things.'

He told me they needed some riveting work done on the top, and some guys that had gone up couldn't take it—it was too high even for them. So I went up, and the cold steel felt strange against my skin and I sensed long tremors in the giant skeleton of the bank, and it was as if the building was alive, shivering, with bones and sinews and tendons, with a life of its own. I didn't trust it, but I went up and up and there was wind all around me. The city seemed to fall away and the voices of the few men who accompanied me sounded strangely hollow and unreal in the high air. There were four of us—a tosser to heat the rivets and throw them to the catcher who caught them in a tin cup and lowered them with tongs into their holes—a riveter who forced them in with his gun, and a bucker to hold a metal plate over the hole. They told me their names as the elevator took us to the top—Joe, Charlie, Amodeo. I was the bucker.

Amodeo offered me a hand when we first stepped out onto a beam, but I couldn't accept it, although the first minute up there was awful. I watched how Amodeo moved; he was small and agile and treated the beams as if they were solid ground. His smile was swift and confident. I *did* take his hand later, but only to shake it after I had crossed the first beam. I kept telling myself that my people were the People of the Eagle, so I of all men should have no fear of walking where the eagles fly, Nevertheless when we ate lunch, the sandwich fell down into my stomach a long long way as if my stomach was still on the ground somewhere, and my throat was the elevator that had carried us up.

I found that holding the metal plate over the rivet holes gave me a kind of support and I was feeling confident and almost happy until the riveter came along and aimed his gun and WHIRR-TA-TA-TAT,WHIRR-TA-TA-TAT! My spine was jangling and every notch in it felt like a metal disc vibrating against another metal disc. After a while, though, I got the knack of applying all sorts of pressure to the plate to counteract some of the vibration. And when the first day was over I was awed to think I was still alive. The next day I imagined that the bank was a huge totem, or the strong man Aemaelk who holds the world up, and I started to like the work.

I didn't see you much those days for I was tired every night, but once I remember we sat over coffee in a restaurant and there was an odd shaky light in your eyes, and you looked sick. A man at a nearby table was gazing out onto the street, dipping a finger from time to time into his coffee and sucking it. I asked you why he was so sad. 'He's not a whale,' you answered.

'Then what is he?' I asked.

'He's a little salmon all the whales are going to eat,' you said. 'Like you, like me.'

'Where are you working now, Aaron?'

'In a sewer. You go up, Lucas, and I go down. It fits. Right now I'm a mole and you're the eagle.'

Aaron, I've got to finish this letter right now. I don't have time to write all I wanted to, because my trial's coming up and I already know how it's going to turn out. I didn't have time to say much about the three years I spent here, about losing the job, about wandering around the city without money, about drinking, about fooling around, about everything falling all around me like the totems falling, about getting into that argument in the tavern, and the fat man who called me a dirty Indian, about how I took him outside into a lane and beat him black and blue and seeing his blood coming out and suddenly he was dead. You know it all anyway, there's no point telling it again. Listen, Aaron, what I want to know now is:

Is my grandfather still telling lies to the history-hunters in Skidegate?

Are the moles and the eagles and the whales coming out of the sewers and subways and buildings now that it's spring?

Have all the totems on my island fallen, or do some still stand?

Will they stick my head up high on a cedar tree like they did to Gunarh?

Will the Street of Walls fall down one day like the totems?

What did you say I would find in the House of the Whale, Aaron? Aaron? Aaron?

FIRE

She stood there, in the smoky emptiness of the place, trying to remember what had happened. It had been more than strange to wake up and see the room—(only yesterday full of books, clothes, tables)—now reduced to a misty void, an uninhabitable region fit only for ghosts. She was thrust back to some point very distant in time; this, she thought, is what the caves of the early men looked like, full of strange chunks of carbon, white ash, charred stumps of nameless things that had once, perhaps, been trees, or bones. . . .

Well, one *does* go a little off the deep end when one finds a house with a real fireplace right in the middle of town. At least the first floor of a house, which is what she had rented only two days ago. Oh, lots of people have fireplaces delicately arranged with brass jars and photographs and woodsy things on the mantelpiece. And those boxes of long long matches that you buy from boutiques and never really use. But nobody ever builds a *fire*, that's the point. Why bother hauling in wood or coal? There's the mess on the rugs, for one thing, and the added problem of where to stack the fuel so it looks decorative as well as functional.

But she had taken the place on the strength of the fireplace alone. When she moved in she had gotten rid of the Kleenexes and cigarette butts and fashion magazines the last tenants had stuffed into the iron mouth, and stood gazing at the black grillwork, which looked now like rows of ferocious teeth. Then she bent down and peered up into the flue—(what a word, *flue*, who gets to use a word like that anymore?)—and imagined that the stars lived not up, but down, very far down at the bottom of the smoky throat of Moloch. Everything the fireplace ate would turn into stars.

Then a whole string of half-remembered words came to mind, words one doesn't use anymore. *Chimney-sweep, stoke, fire-dog, bellows*. And humming happily, she went out into the backyard and broke branches off a tree for two solid hours, brought them back inside and stacked them in front of the fireplace.

Chris was coming that night. They would build one hell of a fire.

She served steaks and salad and Italian bread and wonderful red wine, but they both ate quickly with their eyes darting every now and again to the fireplace with its black mouth so much hungrier than theirs. Like a big iron dog waiting at the foot of the table, killing one's own appetite. Then, as if at some pre-arranged signal, they both got up from the table and emptied their paper plates—(she didn't own any china)—and napkins and even the uneaten pieces of steak, into the fireplace. After a moment's thought she also threw in her one and only tea-towel; it was greasy, and it seemed to her grease was a good thing for starting a fire.

There followed a tremendous bickering about whether the next layer should be composed of twigs or paper. Chris insisted on paper and, not having any on hand, tore up her five year old *Webster's*—(only 95 cents at Coles and easily replaceable)—and threw it in. It was becoming obvious to her that Chris was trying to take over the fire; he kept talking about his hundred camping trips to Gull Lake, and as he threw in the pages of *Webster's* his face had a look of intense concentration. Somewhat peeved, she sat on the carpet and broke twigs loudly. These she stuffed in on top of the paper, surprised that they took up so little space; were they not going to have enough *wood*? she wondered with a slight twinge of panic.

They fought over the box of matches for a few minutes and finally each of them took one and lit separate bits of paper. Within minutes the twigs blazed and died; frantic, Chris put on four medium-sized logs, which immediately went up in a terrible burst of energy. They had to throw in the rest of the wood they had, leaving only one big log she had found near the fence in the backyard.

'We're going to have to think carefully about exactly when to put the log in,' Chris said. 'It has to be late enough so it doesn't smother the coals beneath, and early enough to leave time for the dampness to go out before it can catch fire.'

Chris lit his pipe nervously. 'And once the log's in,' he added, 'there's no more fuel. Damn.'

'Imagine, Chris,' she said, becoming gradually hypno-tized by the flames, 'this is how it was when the pioneers came. And before them, the Indians. This is how they *lived*. Imagine the cold of January, and knowing you had to depend on the fire for everything—cooking, cleaning, heat, even light!'

Chris meanwhile was struggling with an iron knob that closed part of the flue to let the fire burn more slowly. He finally succeeded, and fell back with a sigh. 'True. But after all, you can't go on romanticizing that kind of life.'

'Who's romanticizing it?' she said. 'I was just trying to talk about how *difficult* it must have been.'

'Well, we who have central heating can sit here with our wine and enjoy the fire, just as fire, get it? They certainly couldn't.'

She noticed an ember that had sprung out of the fire like

a little cat, and gingerly took the tongs and placed it back inside. 'Of course not.' She paused. 'Chris, don't you think it's time we put the big log on?'

'Absolutely not,' he said, and set his face in an expression of stubborn refusal. It was obvious he wasn't going to surrender their last piece of wood to Moloch without a fight.

'We're all slaves of our environment,' he put in.

She was reluctant to take up the thread of the conversation; Chris was altogether too ironic, if not cynical, about certain aspects of the human predicament. He regarded free will as a hilarious joke—(of course, she conceded, one is never *free*)—but he carried his modern fatalism a little too far for her liking. They always ended up arguing.

'But to different *degrees*,' she insisted. 'Those people who lived in log cabins half frozen to death *did* something. They gathered fuel until their backs broke, they built *fires*. And little by little they conquered their environment.'

'You're talking about physical environment,' he put in, a little peeved. 'What about *human* environment? If we're not slaves to the weather or the terrain, we're slaves to human weaknesses, fears, mob instincts. And what about *spiritual* environment, for heaven's sake, we're slaves to our superstitions or our gods. And what about—'

'Chris,' she jumped up suddenly. 'Get the log—quick! It's going out!'

She stood there madly fanning the feeble coals with a cotton blouse she had grabbed off the dresser. Chris meanwhile was solemnly ripping pages out of her copy of *The Golden Bough*.

'Never mind,' he said, seeing her startled glance. 'It's out in paperback, I'll buy you a new copy tomorrow.'

She felt a moment's twinge of regret, but the rapidly failing fire was of more immediate importance. She suddenly realized they would have to have something more than paper to put into the fire, and, hesitating only a moment, she threw in the blouse. She was never very fond of it anyway; it was one of the new see-through kind, and she didn't really want to be seen. Which gave her another idea. All those old bits of clothes in the first drawer of the dresser. In a moment she had them bundled in her arms and was tossing them into the fire—which, to her immense relief, was gradually gaining momentum.

Chris at last put the log on top of the heap, gently, as if it were a dead child or a precious *Torah* scroll, and grinned to see that the vapour was being quickly forced out of it by the intense heat of *The Golden Bough* and Leslie's unwanted clothes.

Now they could relax. And there was still some wine left.

'Chris,' she murmured, adjusting the small rug so they both had room to sit. 'Isn't it fascinating to see all life as a *consummation*. I mean a consuming, like the fire consumes. A burning, an energy, a turning of everything into pure heat, or stars.'

'That's what I've been trying to tell you,' he said. 'We are consumed. By hungry forces outside of us, or inside us. We're burned out. We have no chance. We're *eaten up*, by wind, or rain, or other people, or our own inner demons.'

'But then who are *we*?' she cried. 'What is the *we* that's being consumed? Don't you see what I mean . . . *we are* the consuming, *we are* the fire! That's the whole point. The *we* is an *energy*, a *process*, not a thing that's the victim of other energies. Which is why we can never be *slaves* to life; we're partaking of the same energies, always.'

'Darling,' he said, and his voice sounded strangely sad. 'Would you mind awfully if I asked you to do something?'

'Why, Chris, of course not!' she said, her eyes growing large and bright. Had she at last broken the shell of his resistance?

'Would you mind awfully,' he went on, 'If I asked you to

sacrifice this little rug to the fire? Look, the log's not going to last long.'

Well, she thought, it was the first time she had seen Chris so deeply interested in something. And the rug ($2·50 at the local hardware store) was easily replaceable. She got out a strong pair of scissors and, with some effort, they managed to cut the rug in half so the separate pieces would fit into the fireplace.

'This is just like an Indian *potlache*!' Chris exclaimed. 'Some of the West-Coast tribes used to throw their most precious possessions into a big fire to show how wealthy they were.'

'You mean they were wealthy enough to show their utter contempt for what they owned,' she said.

'Yes. Something like that. I'm starting to see the point,' he said, and pulled out his address book from his jacket pocket and threw it into the fire, 'Don't you have the strange feeling,' he went on, untying his tie, 'that it's freezing winter outside and we're living in a huge hostile forest, willing to sacrifice anything, our souls, even, to keep the fire going?'

'I do, sort of,' she said, her arms full of books she'd gathered at random, not even looking at the titles. 'But after all, Chris, it's only October. I mean, we're not going to *die*, or anything, if the fire goes out.'

'I know,' he said, throwing his tie into the fire, 'but I just have this *feeling*.'

They put the books in one by one, without tearing up the pages first. A whole volume gave a nicer light than a pile of crumpled-up pages. Reddish, with wisps of blue from the ink.

She and Chris began to gather up various things from the house and bring them to the fireplace, for they found that if they made many small trips to get something, they felt very chilled.

She had been dubious about the chemical fibres in her brown pant-suit ($28·00 at Eaton's), but to her surprise and delight the semi-synthetic material gave off a wonderful glow. Chris was even more doubtful about his tweed sports jacket. He was sure the wool in it would make a horrible stink—but no, it burned slowly and calmly. Almost as well as the four small Mexican cushions, the sheets and the thin bedspread from the bed. The wooden salad-bowl was a great disappointment; it lay there and took *hours* to go away, but toward the end it gave off a lovely aroma of oil and spices which, when mingled with the fragrance of her cedar jewelry-chest, almost drove them wild.

'I wonder,' said Chris, anxiously peering out of the window, 'if we can hold out till morning.' And his eyes had the quick, watchful, half-savage expression which the early settler must have worn as he gazed out of his cabin on a winter night, looking for wolves, bears, Indians. Or which the Indian must have worn when peering out of his tent by night watching for wolves, bears, white men.

He came away from the window and crouched by the fire. 'Leslie,' he said, 'I want to ask you something important. I want you to give me an honest answer. . . .'

And again she looked up at him, eyes wide with expectation.

He drew a deep breath. 'Leslie, do you *like* your kitchen table? I mean—well, hell, are you *attached* to it? I mean, is it something you could get along without for a day or two? I mean—'

He lost himself in a flutter of words as she silently handed him the axe.

She stood there, in the smoky emptiness of the place, trying to remember what had happened. She was thrust back to some point very distant in time. This, she thought, is what the caves of the early men looked like, full of strange chunks of carbon, white ash, charred stumps of nameless things that had once, perhaps, been trees, or bones. . . .

Well one *does* go a little off the deep end when one finds a house with a real fireplace right in the middle of town.

DAY OF TWELVE PRINCES

The boy Samuel stood by the window and bit his lip just sharply enough to draw blood. He was lean and brown like the lean branch outside, the branch he worshipped at an appointed time each afternoon when the sun touched it tentatively, from the left. The wood became pure gold and Samuel thought; I, I am here in the attic this afternoon and no-one else in the world sees what I see at this time. No-one. Therefore what I see I possess completely—this branch, this sun, this light.

And the sun ran its fingers along the body of the branch, tracing, exploring, transforming it into a warrior's golden bow, a weapon of pure fire, unstrung, divorced from the tree. And Samuel thought: Therefore this fire is also mine and the power that goes with it. It is mine because no eyes but mine perceive it. It is given to me by strange laws I do not need to understand.

And he ran his fingers along the window-pane, tracing the curve of the bow, testing it. Then the sun slipped like melted butter from the bark, and the bow became bough, and it was all over. He sat down on the floor beside an old rusted bird-cage, trying to open the little door that had been closed for years. Powdered red dust lodged beneath his fingernails and awful longings rose up within him. He longed for tangible power, for a bow worthy of princes. The bird-cage wouldn't open, and he pulled and prodded, poked a forefinger inside and tried to jab the hinge, but he caught his fingernail on a wire and sliced off a shiny white half-moon in the attempt. The attic was stuffy—(like a tomb, Sarah always said)—and he wanted to go outside and search for a big bug with golden armour on its back, the kind he had once read about.

Footsteps on the stairway . . . not hard ones like Aubrey's, not worried silky shufflings like Sarah's, but quick light ones, his mother's. She moved like a beautiful forest animal, hunting, her feet scarcely touching the ground. But he wasn't pleased to hear her entering the attic. Hannah didn't understand the bow, or the bird-cage, or anything really. She just floated, hunted, danced. Puffs of dust powdered the air as she pushed the door open.

'I'm looking for some peacock blue silk for cushion covers, Samuel . . . seen any?'

'In the trunk, I guess.'

'Sarah says the yellow cushion covers make her sick. Especially on a red sofa. She says it looks like a circus. Do you think it looks like a circus?'

Samuel imagined white horses tearing up and down the yellow silk, their hooves slicing the cushions open, the room filling with feathers . . . but now Hannah had found the peacock blue silk and was dancing with it around the attic, humming some old gypsy tune under her breath. (*Mother, are we really gypsies?* he had once asked her. And she had nodded *yes, yes we are.*) She was dark as a frown, light as a laugh, yet clear and unambiguous in her dance. Her body seemed made of thousands of tiny springs; her limbs had alarming shapes and angles. Her love, he thought, was like the peacock blue silk, a bright thing draped around her body, a thing worn outside.

When she left, he picked up the little half-moon finger-nail and studied it carefully. 'This is me,' he said aloud. 'And if I put it in the earth then I shall be part of the earth. No one will know that the ground they tread on is a part of my body. I will lie quietly beneath the grass and blend with all of nature. The fingernail will take root and another me will spring from the soil. . . .'

Solemnly, as if in ritual, he buried the fingernail under the great tree in the garden. Then he covered the hole with cool earth and smiled. Each new secret gave him a certain power. The afternoon grew older and the brown bow hung with powerful grace somewhere above him.

'Are you well enough to be downstairs?' Aubrey was asking.

'Of course,' Sarah said, 'I'm not sick, you know, I'm merely living on a higher plane than the rest of you. Occasionally my spirit gains control of my body and forces it to do strange things, but is that so bad?'

Aubrey helped her to sit down, though as always he had the uneasy feeling that she was holding *him*. His wife's tyranny wasn't the tyranny of the sick, the weak. She was neither of these. She was merely mad, and her madness was fourteen years old, as old as Samuel. It involved little more than having hallucinations in the house . . . red bats and yellow vermin, for instance, were always assailing her. It was a flagrant, uncomplicated sort of madness, beneath which there was an area of dreadful sanity. (Dreadful only by contrast? Aubrey wondered.) She was capable of sheer confusion and terrible clarity, wild hallucinations and poignant, cutting perceptions of reality. She had few actual fears, except the fear of open spaces—so the garden was fenced off from the acres of land around. She claimed the fences had a reverse purpose; they were the world-limits, not the limits of her garden; they made prisoners of everyone in the world except those who lived within them.

She was always hungry. The contours of her body itself reminded one of spoons and bowls.

28

Her power was the echo of a distant matriarchy, though she had no child of her own. Her eyes were colourless, but when they caught the light they held and concentrated it into many small sharp points. Sometimes her madness was almost graphic, her face an acute map that seemed to have been drawn by all the explorers that ever were.

Aubrey himself had iron-grey hair and his eyebrows were black wings that threatened to fly away from their ridges of bone. He rarely spoke to the boy Samuel; he usually stared, as if trying to formulate a question, but the question had been forming for fourteen years and Samuel no longer expected it would ever be asked. Samuel often imagined meeting Aubrey on some medieval battlefield with knights and horses and long silver swords. His army was composed of twelve young princes, one for every hour of the day. Aubrey's army was always composed of twelve black riderless horses, one for every hour of the night.

Dinner was strained and silent. Afterwards, the household seemed to decompose. Hannah sewed cushion-covers in her room; Sarah sat reading an ancient issue of *National Geographic*; Samuel disappeared into the garden, and Aubrey poured himself a glass of very dry wine, sat down at his desk and drew three concentric circles on the blotter, gazed out the window at the darkening garden and whistled softly. It might storm.

Sarah ran her fingers through her loose, yellow-grey hair, searching for something, an old thought, a memory hidden at the roots. Hannah smoked a cigarette in the kitchen, running one hand down her beautiful weary hips. She smiled to see Samuel hand Sarah a bright red flower, a wild one he'd found growing alone in the garden. For a moment it seemed as if Sarah was pleased with it, but then she let out a long low moan that climbed the scale to a whine, the night-sound of an animal. She dropped the red flower on the floor and wept and wept. Samuel ran upstairs, where the attic was cool and private, where he felt he was above them all, standing on their heads, rising like the Holy Ghost above their shoulders, where they became Lilliputians and he the master of Lilliput. If he stamped his heels, would he crack their skulls and gain entry into their heads? He stamped softly. For Sarah. He stamped sharply. For Hannah. He stood near the trunk, for Aubrey's room was right below it, and pounded several times with all his might.

Later as he lay in bed he thought of an old green hat he had seen in the attic, lying crushed beside the bird-cage, a wicked, crazy red feather growing out of it like part of a slain bird. The feather raced across his consciousness and a stream of images all involving and not involving the hat sent him off to sleep. He dreamed of Hannah who was wild because her long hair sensed wind everywhere around her, because her long fingers sensed wind when she lit cigarettes; they cupped themselves protectively around the flame.

At midnight thunder woke him and he got out of bed and stood before the black window. Lightning cast bright images of himself against the pane. He saw that he was naked; he looked down the length of his body and saw how truly thin he was—not like a prince, not like a warrior. Naked still, he slipped downstairs to find an apple, a big luscious one, the kind that cracks and squirts when you first bite into it. As he passed along the dark hall the carpet was like thick moss under his feet. A small light issued from the living room; curious, he peered inside. Hannah was dancing again. At midnight. In the middle of a summer thunderstorm. There was no music; there was only her body with its inherent rhythms. He smelt wine. His mother was dancing again, her head tossed back and her wild hair flowing. Without music his mother danced; she must have used the grotesque melodies of the storm. She twirled and twisted through a hundred twirling twisting worlds. She laughed.

'You must be dancing *for* someone . . .' Samuel thought.

And Aubrey lay on the sofa, drowsy with wine, his terrible eyebrows no longer terrible, merely dark curtains for his eyes.

And Samuel saw his own nakedness; in witnessing this dance it was he who had somehow been seen. His inviolable body had been exposed, his dreams, his secrets, everything. He ran back to his room and lay face down in bed. Why did Hannah dance? He wished he owned a bow and arrow, a bow no man but he could bend, an arrow clean and straight as a thought. Why did Hannah dance? At midnight, in a storm, with no music?

The next day he made a bow, and his spirit-father helped him make it, the man with skin brown as bark and eyes like two black suns who, Hannah had told him, was dead somewhere in Europe. Samuel saw him often in his minds' eye— lord of princes. He smiled and a hundred suns rose and set, he rode snowy stallions forever through the deserts of his dreams and carried a long javelin set with a hundred precious stones. He wore large rings on his fingers, his voice was deep and clear, his hand calmed turbulent horses. . . .

Samuel held the bow high and it hovered over the morning like a deadly bird. Inside the house Sarah played dominoes, waiting for Hannah to sweep out the fabulous finger-tall people who, she claimed, had overrun her bedroom. She placed the licorice-black rectangles beside one another in random patterns, laughing all the while slowly and sadly beneath her breath. At three o'clock Aubrey heard a sharp twang outside his study window. He stepped outside into the sunlight and, shading his eyes against the glare, made out Samuel's small form in the bushes at the end of the garden.

'Samuel?'

An arrow buzzed past his ear; he stepped back a pace,

then smiled and picked the arrow up off the porch. It was only a hastily-cut willow branch—why had it frightened him?

At 3.30 Samuel went to the attic, removed three crushed butterflies from his pocket, laid them down in a row and tacked them to the floor with thumbtacks through their wings. He watched them awhile, then thought better of it. He removed the thumbtacks, picked the butterflies up in a heap and felt the unbearable softness of their furry bodies against his skin. He dropped them from the attic window and they fell, they did not fly. Then he cried, covering his face lest his princes witness his shame, and the tears washed away the bow, the sun, the house, the dancing.

Hannah, like most beautiful people, was constantly touching herself, checking to see that all her parts were in order. She ran hands over hips, comb over hair, fingers over eyebrows and tongue over lips from dawn to dusk, keeping that tactile contact with herself, that quiet dialogue with her own body. But, she thought, she missed something, lacked something, something like the taste of strawberries in summer, something like the feel of her skin drinking the sunlight in, something like ankle-high grass. But it was none of these. She pulled a prodigal hair from her eyebrow and tried to pinpoint what it was she wanted. Longer hair? A full skirt with tight bands of elastic to caress her waist? No, no. Wine? Brazil nuts? No, no, no.

She turned then and saw Sarah watching her from the doorway.

That night Sarah put on a tight ruby-red dress with big dyed feathers around the hem. She took an hour to get into it, and the cruel zipper bit her flesh in several places before it consented to close. Now she stood at the top of the stairway and looked down at herself. It was an old dress, a remnant of a dead past; her breasts strained against the worn silk and her swollen stomach had already split some of the seams; little bands of white were exposed beneath the redness. Still she believed she was beautiful and felt sure that the dress had transformed her, that somehow it would command her body to become smooth and firm again. But then, she had no mirrors. Slowly she descended the stairs, and those in the living-room looked up to see her giggling on the threshold; then she spilled into the room like a glass of red wine.

Samuel buried his head deeper into the book he wasn't reading. Sarah's perfume skinned the lining of his nostrils; it was so stringent, medicinal, alcoholic, having no doubt been fermenting for ten years in an old perfume bottle. Sarah's reluctant body swung round and round in a mad dance until the absurd feathers flapped loudly around her legs and the white band of flesh at her waist widened.

Samuel read the same sentence for the fifth time, and Sarah threw off wild smells of mothballs and camphor and antique perfume as she passed him. A few loose sequins fell from her dress in a rain of red and landed on his lap like live things; disgusted, he flicked them off. She flung an arm in the air and sent down another sequin shower upon him. The side seams of her dress split and part of the bodice fell down in a sad flap and exposed a large triangle of white beneath. Sarah was falling apart, like an old tree in autumn, like a dream before dawn.

No-one had noticed Aubrey, but now he rose from his chair, poured two glasses of wine red as blood, red as her dress, crossed the floor, and gave one to her. He clicked his glass against hers and his face, Samuel thought, was composed of layers of masks. 'Sarah, we are getting old,' he said. 'To your red dress, Sarah,' he said. Sarah drained her glass in a moment, reeled a little, and fell forward. Aubrey caught her and put an arm around her waist. No-one spoke. Slowly he led her upstairs.

And Hannah lit a cigarette, hands cupped tightly round the flame, the flame that was threatened by the wind that was suddenly there, in the room. And Samuel went out to lie under the great tree in the garden and drink the night air which purifies, he thought, which heals.

In the bedroom Sarah's red dress magnified her, became the total colour of her madness. Aubrey felt himself being drawn into it, into her, into the vast seas of redness and the strange power of her will. He found himself weeping into the cool turquoise coverlet and the satin pillowslips, and all the while the redness held him, waves of it engulfed him, and then Sarah's body began to follow an old, half-forgotten dance.

Samuel fell asleep under the tree in the garden and it was very late when he awoke and crept back into the house. As he undressed in the darkness of his room, red sequins fell out from the folds in his pants.

Now Sarah's Lilliput people, the red bats and yellow vermin disappeared, or ran off, as she claimed, into the woods. After the night of the red dress she had spiralled or pivoted into sleep and dreamed sweet dreams of her sweet clumsy dancing. And now she was pregnant, and she laughed so much that she decided she would have to call her son 'Laughter.' 'Is there a name that means *laughter*?' she asked Aubrey, and he told her he thought *Isaac* meant laughter. 'Isaac it is,' she said.

Then she decked her hands with dense bracelets and rings, and her touch grew heavy and sure, the ornaments giving her a kind of gravity. And Hannah lit a hundred cigarettes, her hands cupped protectively round the match-flames.

One Saturday Samuel decided to go to the carnival that was in town for the weekend. He stole money from the little red jar in the kitchen and left at dawn before anyone was awake. The early grass was dewy and cool under his feet, the moisture soaking up through the soles of his shoes. The sun heaved up from the horizon with the great red chariot of day behind it, chalking the clouds in wild pastels. Great white horses of light charged across the sky. Soon his arm would be tanned and brown and he would bend the biggest bow in the world, a bow the size of a rainbow. The day grew hotter, but he didn't mind, for he was the heat and the cold and he was the gravel of the road. Soon his twelve princes would join him and pay homage to him and grovel at his feet.

The road tore its way through a thick bush, then opened out. It was almost noon, and the sun hung above him like a gold watch on a chain or a giant pendulum. Indians had walked where he now walked; perhaps he would find an ancient moccasined footprint beside his own, a ghostly companion. Now the road wound lazily like a snake through the yellow grass. Rabbits scuttled away and the day droned in a low drone of bee and bird and bush. Somewhere far away Hannah was pulling in a million miles of laundry from the clothesline that reached to the limits of the world.

'You wanna groom horses for a buck?' asked the man with the cigar. 'Hey kid! You wanna groom hor—'

'No, I want to ride one! That one, the big Arab!' Samuel cried.

'Can't kid. You're not with the *show*. You wanna groom—'

'I'll take it and ride it out of the field and over the river and into the woods, big man!'

'Can't kid. You're not with the troupe. Say, you wanna haul water for a buck?'

'Over the river and way beyond the hills! Think I can't? I got fire!'

35

'You got fire, kid?'

'I got fire.'

'You got parents, kid?'

'I got lots of things.'

'You got sense, kid?'

'I got fire.'

The man with the cigar eyed him steadily, then motioned for him to follow him into the little cabin behind the trailer.

'You wanna ride the Arab, kid?'

'Yeh!'

'You can ride?'

'Yeh!'

'You got spunk, kid.'

The man gave him something that at one time might have been an orange. Outside the cabin the sounds and smells of the carnival charged the air. Cheap red and yellow music tinkled and scraped; horses neighed and the dwarfs and giants and snake-dancers spoke in a hundred tongues. Somewhere outside in the fenced-off area behind the tent the Arab pawed the ground.

'What if I let you have a go at him for an hour. . . . Will you do some grooming later on?'

'Yeh!'

And the man led him out into the field where the Arab waited, and Samuel sprang up onto its great back. He felt a great heartbeat against his knees as his legs hugged the beast; he felt great boat-ribs heaving against the flesh of his inner thighs. Arab's flank was hot and sticky; he took off and worked up to a full gallop almost instantly. His white body sucked the wind, his tail was a streak of horizontal light. Wind cracked against Samuel's face, wind that he and the horse created with their speed, and he crouched low over the Arab's back, thrilling to the beat of the huge heart between his legs.

A wild idea seized him and, scarcely pausing to consider the danger, he urged the Arab on to one end of the field, where the fence looked low enough to jump. He could hear the man calling out for him to stop, but he didn't care; they cleared the fence in one fluid leap and found themselves free in the fields beyond. Samuel buried his face in Arab's mane and he knew himself to be a part of the beast; he was a centaur, and everything from his chest down was pure horse. The carnival fell back behind him, the sugary smells of the booths, the costumes, the freaks. The Arab knew his darkest thought, the Arab was an arrow shot from his desire, seeking its target. He spoke to the horse, he whispered, 'Don't stop, don't stop, go right through these trees, these fields, this forest, don't stop until something is made clear between us, 'til this race makes something true in me, 'til we've drawn a long white line of light from the carnival to the ends of the earth. . . .'

But the tension in the horse's body slackened and he tired and became a thing once more separate from the boy. They rested in a field, and the Arab's wet head curved down like some great terrible swan to taste the grass. Samuel lay on the thick turf and laughed. 'I am the earth, the turf, the trees, the fibres of fire in the Arab's body. . . .'

It was almost dusk when they turned onto the road that led home. He imagined his mother fixing strawberries, her hands all stained with their sweet red blood, taking them one by one and cutting off their little green heads and throwing their bodies into a bowl. Then she threw in sugar like snow and covered them all in snowy graves. He could almost taste their sweetness; his mouth watered, and he was exhausted. The Arab's flank chaffed mercilessly against his legs. He collided with a cluster of butterfles and their wings clouded his vision. A car was approaching from not far off. The Arab worked up to a full gallop and swerved off to the side of the road. It was Aubrey's car, Samuel was sure of it now. He dug his fingers into the Arab's neck but the strained and corded muscles beneath were bent on their own task. Now the car stopped and Aubrey waved madly from the window. Then, incredulous, he got out and stood by the roadside, shading his eyes against the last slanting rays of the sun. The Arab headed straight for him, and at the last minute, not ten feet away, neighed shrilly and reared back, his front hooves chopping the air. The proud head dripped with sweat and flew wildly back and forth as if in laughter.

At that moment Samuel slid off his back, his knees unable to clutch the beast any longer. He caught a glimpse of Aubrey's face. He wanted to smile then, to laugh, but the ground heaved up to meet him and darkness came. The Arab whinnied once, then shot off into the bush.

He thought he heard a high thin sound, like the sound the sun makes when it rises, like the scraping of fingernails against a window-pane. He imagined he smelled thunder at the edge of the woods and it smelled thick and brown like meat. He imagined the sound of lightning between two clouds, slicing and piping like a piccolo. For days all his senses were confused. The room was big around him; it was as if he looked at it through a telescope. By night the trees were borne down with dark rain and thunder lay like a blanket on the earth. Large wet leaves pasted themselves onto the window-pane like the hands of curious children peering into a haunted house. The great tree in the garden emptied its skirts occasionally and buckets of rainwater fell out and some large branches went flop, flop.

When I fell, he thought, *I pulled all the glory with me to the ground.*

The whole house was pregnant like Sarah, waiting to let loose something dark, unspeakable. And when Sarah had the child they would all be born, or die.

I do not hear the evil door closing behind Aubrey and Hannah as they go into her room. I do not hear the rustle of clothes, the thick whispers. I do not hear the flick of the match or the creak of the bed. Nothing is heard, nothing. I do not hear their voices, I do not hear Hannah's fingernails as she draws them across the wooden dresser-top. I hear nothing, I have never heard them in that room ... he told himself.

And he heard Aubrey's low voice saying, 'Some part of him knows everything, some part of him has heard every word we have ever spoken ....'

No, I hear nothing. Father, I hear nothing, he said.

One night long after, Sarah seemed to be growing bigger and bigger like Alice in Wonderland; she thought her head would go clear through the ceiling and her feet poke holes in the walls. She dreamed of an enormous loaf of bread that had been baking in an oven for hundreds of years; she dreamed of a great red tulip with the petals folded back; she dreamed that she had swallowed her little girl-self and now after many years it was struggling to escape; she dreamed of a set of abacus beads she had owned as a child, beads of many colours, and of her own tiny hands pushing them up and down the taut wires, making obscure calculations long since forgotten. And the very next day when Samuel passed Sarah's room there was a white man and a white lady inside and through the half-open door he caught a glimpse of the white man holding something squigly and red in the air. He went downstairs and filled a large bucket of water and carried it outside, and the bucket was suddenly heavy; he carried tears, water, bows and arrows, rocks and stones, flowers, years, everything. The sun painted a bright yellow arc across the sky; the trees were all burning, each one a Moses bush; rocks were like mirrors throwing off the light, and the birds were all albinos. There was no sound, no sound at all, and then everything lost its colour and became white, white. Slowly but surely the sun was changing its direction, turning and going backwards, becoming a pendulum. And he thought he was walking backwards into the house and taking the water bucket back to the sink where the water was sucked back into the faucet; then he was walking backwards upstairs and seeing the squigly red thing again, and returning to his bed, and going back fourteen years until by a strange magnetism he was sucked back into the body of Hannah. And then there was darkness.

It was a grey day, steel grey like a shark's back. Thunder was suggested. Aubrey went to the attic.

'What's the password?' came a voice from the shadows.

'Excalibur,' Aubrey guessed.

'Wrong!'

'Hyperboreas.'

'Wrong again.'

'Fimbul winter.'

'You may enter.'

Samuel was whittling a piece of wood, worrying it into an arrow. The bow lay on the floor between them.

'Why don't you do this downstairs?' Aubrey asked.

'Too messy, I get shavings on the floor.'

Aubrey crouched down low beside the boy and played with some of the shavings. *I wish I could grow backwards*, he thought, *I wish I could grow young again.*

Samuel said nothing. A few grains of pipe tobacco had fallen from Aubrey's pocket, and he wanted to crush them under his heel like ants. He whittled silently, furiously, faster and faster until the arrow point was fine and sharp as a truth, or a poignant word. Without asking, Aubrey took it from him and turned it over and over in his fingers. He inspected it from all angles; he poked, he pried, and Samuel thought it was his soul there in Aubrey's hands being examined until there was no niche left unexplored, no part of

40

its surface left untouched. He was just about to cry out in protest when he noticed that the buttons of Aubrey's shirt were all done up wrongly—one out each time. And a spider was slowly crawling up his sleeve and he didn't notice it. When it reached the collar, Samuel sprang forward and flicked it away; he found his arm locked in a vice, and Aubrey was holding onto him tightly, crying.

He hadn't asked for this, he hadn't made the first move; he felt himself violated like the piece of whittled wood, seized, taken, something being asked of him, something he couldn't give. He wrenched his arm away, surprised at his own strength. 'No!' he cried. 'You can't have me, I'm not *you*!'

The last word hung in the air as Aubrey turned away and walked to the attic door, his shoulders sloping, his walk slow and numb.

'Your buttons are all done up wrong,' Samuel whispered after him, but Aubrey didn't hear.

The last thing he remembered about the house was the way Isaac sat on the ground in the garden, picking up bits of the world around him—grass, pebbles, leaves. The universe for him was a gigantic jigsaw puzzle; all its parts were there, waiting to be pieced together.

Sarah had slowly come to lose her fear of open spaces and even allowed the occasional flower to be brought into the house. She turned Hannah and Samuel out, telling Aubrey she could endure them no longer, and Aubrey didn't protest. He gave Hannah money, and an address in the city, and she cried, 'You don't remember anything—the promises, the strawberry-coloured negligée, the dances!'

'Be good to the boy,' he said to her, and then he cried.

'Ha!' Hannah yelled after him. 'Ha!'

Before they left, Samuel paid a last visit to his favourite spot by the river. In the distance the city lay, hot and grey and metallic on the horizon. Then later, as the train pulled away, he wondered if perhaps he shouldn't have embraced the man he knew to be his father—just once, in fourteen years. He thought of the strange magnetism of the great tree in the garden, the way it lured the sunlight into its branches, stole the sunlight, shone. He thought of himself walking backwards into the house and upstairs, placing a spider on Aubrey's collar and slowly, painstakingly, placing a thousand slivers of wood back onto the arrow until it was a branch again.

But the big doors of the house were closed behind them. Inside, Aubrey and Sarah and a child called Laughter were putting up balloons and taking down balloons and laughing and crying forever and ever.

The city had no winged sphinx at its entrance, no riddle and no reward. He hated the first people they stayed with. They owned two fierce canaries and ate sliced ham and Waldorf salad every day of the week. Hannah hated them too, so they left and wandered from place to place with their money running out and Hannah unable to find work. Finally they found a place in the east end of the city, a single room in a dark damp house. The darkness in the place was an intrinsic darkness; it had nothing to do with the weather outside. Sun licked the walls, seeking entrance in vain; every day was a stormy day and every day it rained within the house.

Samuel hated the city, but there was a market-place nearby where everything in the world was on sale, even, it seemed, the countless children who played there, children whose parents had come from Naples and Warsaw and Malta and Macedonia and Pakistan and Dachau. There were little Romans riding bikes, little Greeks making odysseys to the fruit man who gave them free oranges and pears, little remnants of European Jewry playing solemn games, wearing long coats and kinky curls in front of their ears. One day he asked someone if they knew the way to Howland Street, by way of starting a conversation, and the boy—Yehudi—replied, 'Certainly I know the way to Howland Street.' Then the pale studious face turned away. 'Then how do I *get* to Howland Street?' Samuel pressed. 'You're almost *standing* on Howland Street,' Yehudi answered solemnly. 'I mean, I live there ...' Samuel went on. 'So do I,' said Yehudi. 'That's how I know where it is.' They gazed at each other a long while and finally Samuel chuckled and hit Yehudi playfully on the shoulder, but Yehudi's liquid black eyes showed no amusement. 'You know where Howland Street is too,' he said, 'if you live there.'

'Well, I'm still sort of new around here.'

'You're new, ah, you're *new* ...' and Yehudi leaned forward confidentially. 'Then you'd better take care who you hang around with. Gangs around here. Goodbye.' And Yehudi disappeared among the baskets of purple and green grapes. Someone was crying, 'I got everything! Shoes, glassware, cheese, fine YELLOW pears good LEATHER-ware potsandpans drapery!' and a rival across the street shouted, 'You get here I got GREEN apples and oranges JAFFA fresh fish—'

'... wickerbaskets HANDmade, salami and all kinds meats LOW price fish LIVE crabs—'

Samuel had no money but he felt he owned it all, the discordant market, its smells, its people ... and soon he came to like Howland Street, even Howland Street with its alleys full of rubbish and children's thrown-off shoes, with the walls that leaned to kiss each other, with the smell of melting tar in the heat.

Hannah saw that Samuel was thin and his thinness was her thinness, so she took a job in the market selling textiles, and she sold them well, for she would drape the colours around her body and twirl around the shop and the fat old ladies dreamed they might look like Hannah if they bought.

Behind the house and in the alleyways where persistent hollyhocks grew, and in the narrow streets, Samuel sought out Yehudi. He found him one day in the market beside a vat of salted fish, and Yehudi wore horrid purple corduroy trousers and a big cap; he had a ball in one hand and an apple in the other and was doing a little idle juggling when Samuel approached him. 'Still looking for Howland Street?' he asked. 'It's two to your left.'

'I know it is,' Samuel said.

Yehudi toyed some more with the ball and apple. 'So you're Jewish?' he asked.

'No.'

'But you're new.'

'Yes.'

'Gangs around here for everything, for Portuguese, for Italian, for Jewish and for New,' warned Yehudi.

They stood awhile in silence.

'So do you want to play ball?' Yehudi asked, and handed him the apple.

They went into a little park and tossed the apple and ball back and forth for an hour or so, and it was a kind of dialogue. Then when it got dark they walked slowly back to Howland Street. Yehudi initiated him into the unwritten codes of the district, words that were taboo, people whom one should avoid, streets one should avoid at certain times and so on. And Samuel followed the garish purple corduroy trousers through the violet wash of the twilit streets; they passed the copperware shop, the big-bellied green-glass bottles, the sleek alleycats and the newspapers and another day torn up and thrown on the pavement, the countless salamis dangling from hooks, the blind ragman and his incoherent cry, 'Ooool RAHGS nee RAHGS oooo,' and the huge white horse that pulled his cart homeward, the old man who sat on the curb whittling, the worried shavings piling up at his feet. . . .

44

'What's wrong?' Yehudi was asking. 'What's wrong . . .?'

The blind ragman was following them down the street, and the big horse wore blinkers so it too was blind, in a way.

'What's wrong?' Yehudi was asking, and it was almost dark now and his purple trousers were almost black.

'Once I rode a horse like that . . . no, not like that—a real horse, an Arabian. . . .'

'Really, really!' Yehudi cried.

Then the ragman and the blinded horse turned a corner and were gone. And in a moment Yehudi also was gone, and Samuel took a short-cut home through a dark alley. He heard a scuffling of feet behind him, and he turned and saw a dozen dirty boys brandishing sticks and stones.

'Here are my twelve princes,' Samuel thought, knowing it wasn't that way at all.

They made little noises as they closed in; they bore down slowly, thirsty for battle, for a thousand other thirsts could not be quenched in the world of Howland Street. Samuel realized he had never learned to fight, not really. 'Arab,' he cried. 'Aubrey!' he cried, just before the darkness closed in like a monk's hood around his head.

He dreamed one dream against the pavement; another dream followed, its images reversed. He was riding a white horse on a merry-go-round that went backwards and around him Hannah and Sarah and Aubrey stood, eating mountains of candy-floss, only they ate it backwards, and their speech was incoherent.

Soon the sun would rise in the east, or the west, which-ever the case would be, and Hannah would come looking for him and they would go backwards or forwards, which-ever the case would be. . . . But to his surprise he woke up alone, and found that it was morning. And as he stumbled along toward Howland Street, second to the left, he heard a sound of laughter in the alleyway—wild laughter, sharp laughter, the laughter of children, the kind you hear at carnivals. And when he turned around he saw twelve princes, one for every hour of the day, and their golden bows lay on the ground before them, and they held twelve white flags of surrender to the sun.

THE OARSMAN AND THE SEAMSTRESS

She thought if she didn't get the dress started that day she'd go mad. Or maybe she wouldn't, which would be worse. The great piece of dark red velvet had been waiting for weeks to become something, to assume a form, and she felt it could wait no longer. So she laid out the material on the floor and rummaged through a drawer for an old pattern, an incredibly complicated pattern even though it was made by Simplicity. When she found it, she was surprised to find how chewed-up and rumpled it was; had she used it *that* many times, she wondered. Probably, since all the dresses she made had a habit of falling apart after a couple of weeks. All her clothes were so ephemeral and she'd dreamed for many years of one day creating the ultimate dress, something she could wear forever and ever, with seams not sewn but welded together.

But everybody knows about velvet. It wears down easily and goes shiny in all the strategic places. Never mind, she'd do it anyway.

Constantine was still asleep, and she hoped the rustling of the paper pattern wouldn't wake him. She loved to watch him while he slept, perhaps because in his sleep he no longer possessed himself, he was a lost being, a kind of orphan, suspended in another time and connected only by the thinnest of threads to his own consciousness. She loved to watch him while he slept, perhaps because it was then that she could enjoy the illusion of actually knowing him. Knowing him in his *otherness*, his state of being other than her. His sleep alienated her and paradoxically, drew her closer to him.

And he always told her about his dreams.

Why is it only women are supposed to be beautiful? she thought as she smoothed out the pieces of the pattern over the dark red velvet. How come Rossetti or Browning couldn't *describe* the man they loved, only their own reactions to him?

Constantine was making little noises of protest in his sleep. She wondered, as she began to tack down the pattern to the velvet, if he was dreaming again of the great Byzantine ship with the golden bird at the bow, and if he were once again among the dying, sweating men in the galley manning the oars, rowing their leaders to some barbaric shore. Then Constantine turned in the bed, slowly, as if in sleep his weight had somehow increased, and the sheets slipped way from his fine knees and thighs and he lay there unprotected, warm with dreams. Accidentally she jabbed a pin into her hand at the sight of his beautiful body. I cannot possess him, she thought. I cannot possess anything. *But he tells me his dreams.*

She finished mooring the bits and pieces of the pattern to the velvet and surveyed the result, like a pioneer proudly surveying the land he has staked out for himself. Then she began to tackle all the blasted cryptic symbols on the pattern. She never could make them out, all those dotted lines and heavy lines and lines that said PLACE ON FOLD and lines that said CUT HERE and little black triangles which for some reason said nothing at all because you were supposed to know that you had to match them up with other little black triangles. Who were the mad geniuses of the Simplicity Pattern Company who made things so

48

damned complicated? She had never in her life attempted a Vogue or McCall pattern, because they were only for people with IQ's of over 150.

She began thinking of the pile of old clothes in her closet, things from years back that she couldn't throw away because she'd worn them on certain Important Occasions. Perhaps one day she would cut a patch from each, and make a patchwork quilt, and she and Constantine would sleep beneath the thousand costumes of her life.

She got out her pinking shears, rather frightening things really. When she'd first bought them she'd gone mad and charged around the house pinking everything in sight, curtains and papers and tableclothes and towels. For a moment now she had a strong desire to take the shears and go to Constantine's bed and silently pink all around the edges of his sheets and pillowcases. To decorate his sleep. Because his sleep was all she understood, all that was hers. Often when she awoke before him she quietly surrounded the bed with all the things of his world, all the things he liked best—grapes and cigarettes and a comb and coffee and his favourite book and his set of shiny red dice. Today, though, she wasn't going to surround the bed with anything. He was rowing in the galley of the great Byzantine ship, and he would be there for some time.

She thought about the dress. She wanted to make it so that there was no point where it really closed, no zippers or buttons or hooks or any of those awful things people invented when they forgot how to make their robes hold together with a single golden buckle or a mere wisp of a belt.

The men in the galley of the Byzantine ship wore nothing at all, perhaps only a loin-cloth. They didn't think much about their bodies, only the pain of their bodies. And their women waiting and weeping for them on distant shores didn't think much about their bodies either; they thought more about their own female bodies and the day their men would come home and praise them.

Damn it, I'm not going to make a dress, she thought. It's him that should be adorned, it's him who's sweating and slaving away in that steaming galley.

So she took away all the little pins that held the pattern to the cloth and once again the dark red velvet lay there waiting to assume a form. I'll make him a shirt, she thought, a beautiful shirt with gold cord at the cuffs, and he can wear it when his terrible voyage is over, for when he gets off that ship he'll be very cold.

But she didn't have a pattern for a shirt, so she pondered and pondered and finally decided she could do it out of her head, providing she could take some basic measurements while he slept. If she was very quiet and careful.

This is ridiculous, she thought, as she got out her measuring tape and stole over to the bed. Imagine—if he knew what I was doing now. Worse still, what if the *other* men knew? What if his ship-mates knew that at that very moment his woman was standing over him with her measuring-tape to take measurements for a shirt? My God, they'd laugh him down to the depths of the Aegean. I hope they don't see me, she thought. They wouldn't understand.

She managed to measure one arm, and then somehow she got all involved thinking about the narrowness of his chest. He really was a small man, yet his parts fitted together so well the total effect was one of great stature. And as always when she saw him like this, she ran her hand lightly down the strong lyrical line of his side, beginning just under the arm and ending at the bone on his ankle, which jutted out like a wing. He was turned away from her so she couldn't watch his breathing nor see the intricate pattern of his ribs and the muscles of his abdomen, an anatomy so breathtakingly different from her own.

He was sweating slightly as he lay there, probably from

the effort of handling those great booming oars. But he seemed relaxed. Perhaps the cruel captain of the ship had given the oarsmen a break. Perhaps enough wind had risen to fill the sails, and now the men were having their daily ration of beer and cheese and salty fish. Perhaps all they had was a bowl of horrible gruel. She desperately hoped it wasn't that. He'd be famished when he woke up. All that bad food they serve on those Byzantine ships.

Suddenly she realized that if she tried to sew anything today she'd go mad. Or maybe she wouldn't, which would be worse. So she threw off her housecoat, took the great piece of dark red velvet and quietly climbed into bed beside him. Then she gently eased all the sheets and blankets off the bed and onto the floor, and covered her naked body and his naked body with the dark red velvet.

Is there room for a woman on your ship? she whispered into his ear. *I'll stow away, no-one will see me, I'll be hidden by dark red velvet. Take me with you, Constantine.*

KINGSMERE

To the north are the Laurentians; to the west, the valley of the Ottawa river; to the south, the capital. He lived here with a dog, some sheep, some bees (until the bears attacked them) and a portrait of his mother reading a book by firelight. When she was alive, she used to visit him, and an observer once wrote that he saw a stagecoach sweep by with a strange beautiful lady in it, and she reminded him of the Queen of the Fairies. And after her death she still visited him—her stagecoach and her silvery voice passing through the great Arch that separates life and death, crossing the Noman's land of time.

Hanging from the beams of the verandah was an ancient bell from a wrecked Nova-Scotian ship; at the main entrance there were two oil lamp standards from Berlin (Ontario) where he was born, and

Arranged around the grounds were the synthetic ruins that still stand today—little walls and terraces and arches, which he made from a strange assortment of historic stone—from the Parliament Buildings, which burned during the First World War, from the doorway of the Bank of British North America, which stood on Wellington Street, from the Houses of Parliament at Westminster and from who knows where else. He reassembled these broken bits of history to frame or emphasize certain aspects of the landscape. He made naked windows and doors for the forest and the hills.

You stand on a terrace flanked by a row of unreal Grecian columns. You look through a classic arch and see, not Athens, nor Rome nor even Palmyra, but the green Gatineau hills of Kanada. You wonder if the landscape protests these borrowed histories, these imported ruins. You wonder if the stones and pillars and arches rest easy here. By day people come to drink tea in the gardens where the house once stood. Few come here by night.

King loved the instruments of time. He wouldn't make an important decision unless the hands of his watch formed a straight line or a neat right-angle. He had a sundial in his garden, which (he wrote) 'not only suggests, but is irrefutable evidence of a perfect order and a complete harmony in all that pertains to Time and Space throughout the physical universe.' He went on to say that 'if such an order exists in Nature . . . is it conceivable, is it rational to believe that underlying the social relations of men and nations an order is not discoverable, obedience to which will bring as perfect a harmony? The sundial reveals to us that, in the physical universe, *position* is the secret to the discovery of design.'

I mean that by night it's quite different. It's not a quaint picnic spot where one might drink tea and muse about the eccentric old gentleman who was once the Prime Minister of Kanada. You stroll across the black grass toward the gardens. The faint light from the tea-house kitchen allows you to make out the shimmering outlines of the arches and the walls. Behind them somewhere are trees, forests, vanished trails of Indians. . . .

He once wrote a letter to a little South-African girl who had asked him about Indians. *The Minister of the Interior says that if he is still Minister of the Interior (you can never be* quite *sure), he will see to it that we have a good supply of Indians on hand . . . now is it true, Elizabeth, that when you have tea in your garden, lions sometimes come and sit down beside you?*

You walk farther down, toward the interior of the garden. Something isn't right. Into whose future are you moving? The wind (are you dreaming) seems to change direction. You forget why you have come here; you make no move to return. You have spotted one very large arch at the far end of the field, and for a second you have an intense, blinding perception of the real nature of the place. This stone on stone, this reconstruction of a past that was never yours, this synthetic history. Only the furtive trees are real; they are the backdrop for an abandoned Greek theatre where the central paradoxes of man were once performed by actors wearing grotesque masks. The insane, incongruous pillars glimmer grey and pearlgrey in the halflight. Here there is a tension between past and future, a tension so real it's almost tangible; it lives in the stone, it crackles like electricity among the leaves.

He tried to transplant Europe, to bring it here among the stark trees and silent trails, but

There, beyond the arch, is the forest. There is the naked, ancient door. You have only to pass under the arch to be free, to be away from this place, but you watch the arch and grow afraid, for the arch is watching you. The little King and the Fairy Queen are watching you. And all the trees are silently screaming.

THE SECOND COMING OF JULIAN THE MAGICIAN

I

'The son of God is dead, which is worthy of belief because it is absurd. And when buried he rose again, which is certain because it is impossible,' said Tertullian. Words that might well apply to me, for in my last life in Europe I was crucified by a bunch of drunkards and peasants in a small village. Quite absurd. (I recall they used leather strips instead of nails.) It was all due to my fatal resemblance to the Nazarene worker of wonders who had preceded me by some two thousand years, and my fatal flirtation with the magic of that ancient mountebank. I did not, however, arise on the third day as he is reputed to have done, but somewhat later.

I, Julian the magician, returned to earth on the birth date of Mithras, the 25th of December in the year 1970. I materialized at noon, in fact, on a ferris-wheel in a second-rate carnival, which was frozen up for the winter, with three white balloons in my left hand and an inverted crucifix made out of red and green tinsel paper stuck to the middle of my forehead.

I allowed myself a moment or two to get my bearings.

That I was no longer in Europe was obvious; I smelled no break baking in ovens, heard no carts jogging down the road. That I was no longer in the nineteenth century was also obvious; for there was a wheezing and a clattering and a grinding all round me from a myriad unseen machines. A car pulled into the parking lot that served as the carnival's winter home; the driver stepped out, wished me a Merry Christmas and invited me to a shot of whisky from a flask in his glove-compartment.

The balloons and the tinsel paper floated away from my hands and forehead; the wheel of the ferris turned a half-turn and neatly deposited me at the bottom. I got off, shook the snow from my cloak, stamped my boots together once or twice, for my feet were frozen, spoke and found my words inscribed in white steam in the air.

'Thank you. And a Merry Mithrasmas to you,' I said.

The whisky warmed my blood, my boots, my velvet cloak. I knew I had arrived.

I spent the first little while making up for lost time; I read about Kellar and Thurston and Crowley and Blackstone and Houdini, and found myself irresistibly in sympathy with the latter, who had to maintain over and over that his powers were *not* supernatural—(an expert asking him, 'Can you prove it?'). Nevertheless, there hadn't been another Julian during the century of my Sleep, of that I was sure. Someone wrote a book describing the events of my last life. Ah, but the swiftest movement of my left hand as it drops the ball or coin into the *servante* is more evocative than ten pages of prose! And who can tell the world more than I have told in the golden pages of my silence?

I learned very quickly that as long as I lived in North America, I had a choice between performing in carnivals or cheap burlesque halls, neither of which appealed to me very strongly. My audiences were invariably composed of Philistines, my talents ignored. But soon I realized that I was secretly acknowledged in a hundred more subtle ways; I was sleeping deep in North America's subconscious beneath layers of comic books and dreams. In the comic books my cloak is red, green or yellow; there are little wings on my boots, little wings on my head, lightning bolts or sacred hammers in my fists. Only the children worship me now. Atman, his identity hidden only by a 'B' at the beginning of his name, exclaims, 'You can't destroy my laboratory, Dr. Zero, because it's only a duplicate laboratory, whereas my real laboratory is in capsule state beneath my right thumbnail! And you, not possessing the handy Laboratory Diminishing Fluid, have failed to capsulize *yours* in time!'

And Dr. Zero, his identity hidden only by the strange nebulous question-mark that always hovers in front of his face, answers, 'Ah ha! But what I possess under my *left* thumbnail can, when released, destroy the *world!*'

The fiendish laughter fades to silence; my green eyes send the children to sleep, my winged boots fly through their dreams. But I, the master of illusions, have few illusions left. Reality belongs to him who can make and break his dream, who can cause the sun to rise and set at his command, *knowing* his command is but a gesture or a noise. Yet still I wave this wand like a sarcastic tongue at the cosmos until it brings forth a silken sea of scarves representing every level of the spectrum, produce myriads of cards and coins from these tired, intelligent fingers, know myself to be both icon and iconoclast. . . .

I am the primitive machinery that grinds beneath the gears and cogs of your world, O Philistines, and my name is the same from eternity to eternity. Even now when the dark streets and the grey winters overtake me I remind myself that I am the freest of men, for I shape the cosmos according to my pleasure. And no more will I allow the succubus of my art to climb the ladder of my spine and suck out my brain; no more will my beautiful skull resemble a piece of old cheese bored with the hundred holes made by the desperate fiend of my imaginings. The scarred flesh of my stigmata has regrown; I of all men no longer need the bloody signatures of sacrifice on my body. I race toward another, better death. . . .

I worked in three different burlesque houses during the first year. I got exactly seven minutes of performing time between 70-minute marathons of strippers and exotic dancers. During my acts no-one swooned; no-one approached me afterwards with nervous diseases for me to cure. (How very different from my last life when the peasants regarded me as holy man, a healer. But then this is North America. Could Christ have taught in Rome?) I did, at least, possess myself, as did the nearly naked dancers whose very flesh was their own inpenetrable armour against the world. Men came for the thrill of coloured lights playing upon flailing flesh, and my magic served only, at best, to wither the organs of their want. I ought to have produced for them great pink elephants, cloudy mammals of their memory, gold and green Edens, marvellous rain-slick jungles, brown limbs throbbing in seas of moss. . . .

Computers analyse the spectra or stars. But in my heart, the data of a thousand worlds. . . .

Once I was shuffling my cards and letting them fall gently, like rain down my sleeve, and I heard a low chuckle coming from somewhere in the audience. A dark kind of laughter, a groan or a curse. I looked out into the sea of bored faces beyond the footlights. Who had dared to laugh?

'There is one among you,' I said, as the cards collected themselves in my left palm. 'Who disbelieves what I do.'

Again the laughter.

So I let go.

The Jack and Ace of Spades issued from my right ear, the King and Queen of Hearts leaped out of my left, the proletariat of the deck squeezed themselves out of my tie-clip, the Joker slid out of my ribs like a subway transfer, the Jack of Clubs got combed out of my hair, I casually allowed three ping-pong balls to roll out of my pant cuffs, I produced a rabbit from my left shoe, converted it into the Jack of Hearts and swallowed it, I flung the entire deck out into the audience where it became a flock of screaming gulls, and then I walked offstage without a word.

The manager raised my salary. I promptly quit. I spent the next lean week browsing in a mystical library, where a white-haired witch of 70 tried to interest me in Blavatsky. She told me I had the eyes of a Seeker of Wisdom and that I should give myself over to meditation on the Infinite. I informed her I *was* the Infinite. She invited me to attend her lectures on Neo-Mesmerism. I declined. She said my face revealed that I was destined to bring havoc upon the world.

'Whose world?' I asked.

Last week I made a final stand in a burlesque theatre. I did an old trick the Nazarene had known, which I myself had done countless times in my last life in Europe. From a bucket of wet clay I produced a multitude of sparrows. The theatre echoed with the sound of their wings. I let them fly from my hands like wishes, like wild gifts for I don't know who. I felt the blood dancing once again in my veins, I felt myself able to take the clay and shape a Golem or a whole new world. My laughter, pure and clear, rang through the hall, but from the people there was no sound, no sound at all. The scarlet curtain fell like a great weary eyelid, and it was some days before the birds, one by one, disappeared from the theatre and alit on the telephone poles and eaves-troughs of the city, where, I imagine, they eavesdropped on the mad dialogues of men.

Now that it's summer I've entered the carnival, this place of broken tongues, this palace of vertigo. I give the people what they want—the vulgar red and yellow magics, the hilarious swift and frenzied magic that children and fools delight in. I compete with freaks whose hideous bodies capture the attention of the crowds faster than my sleight-of-hand. The barkers, the insane ferris wheels, the tinsel music—all distract my audiences from my performance. They eat hamburgers and candy and sugar floss while I work.

Yesterday Sleeda the Snake Woman sat down beside me, one of her pets draped around her shoulders like a stole. 'You're so mysterious, you never say anything,' she complained. 'Neither do you,' I countered. 'My snakes speak for me,' she answered. 'You speak with your hands.'

'What do you believe, Medusa?' I asked her. 'What is the meaning of the carnival?'

She threw back her head and laughed with such rough gaiety that her pet slipped gently down from one shoulder. '*Meaning!*' she cried, 'What do you mean?'

'Why use the word, Medusa, if you don't know what it means?'

'Well, what do you *mean*?' she cried, and gathered up her limp snake and went away. A giant Eve with beasts, the chapter Genesis in the bible of the carnival.

Here is the dream-chaos where one can go mad for hours without anyone questioning his sanity, where each freak and performer is a kind of mirror no-one has to acknowledge out loud. And at the end of the day the people wander into the real House of Mirrors and watch their bodies take on the crazy contours of monsters. For a moment then, laughing at themselves in the mirrors, they are at one with the meaning of the carnival. Sometimes I watch them posing in front of the big mirror outside the Mirror House. Some don't smile; these I watch more closely. Last week I went in myself, but all the mirrors threw back accurate images of me, undistorted clear. I am already the distorter, I am already the mirror.

Last night I dreamed the carnival was empty and it was once again winter. I walked through deep blue snow and there was a faint ringing sound all round me as the carnival wheels and the carnival machinery contracted in the cold. The blue snow got into my boots and I whispered, 'I want to re-create all of this,' and I stared at the naked ferris and the naked canvas tents. Behold, I was cold and excellent in the naked carnival. I passed my hand before the great wheel frozen in its own vertigo—I passed it once, twice and slowly the machinery groaned and scraped, the metal protested and sang out, and the wheel began to turn. Blue snow clung to its ghostly spokes and blue snowflakes fell like confetti. The wheel turned and its turn was *re*turn; it spun backwards in time through a thousand summers. 'I can bring it all back,' I whispered, as the blue snow began to melt inside my boots. I wore dark blue and silver, I wore white, miraculous gloves ... my frozen breath took shape and a hundred white figures emerged from my mouth to populate the carnival. Once I breathed particularly deeply and a gigantic figure materialized before me. Behold, I had created the Fat Woman.

'Who are you?' I asked, taken aback.

'Reality,' she said, 'But you can call me Reali for short.'

She hung around me and refused to move. She examined my clothes, my wand, my blue and silver cloak, amused. She had every possible variety of body odour known to man. Eventually she waddled away, chuckling to herself, her flesh rippling the surface of a sea.

Now it was midsummer and the snow melted into the sawdust. I wandered into the midway, which was midway beween my awakening and my dream. Suddenly the sky darkened as if an eclipse were taking place. The ferris wheel ground to a halt. All my people disappeared; there was only me and the darkness and the tin music. I began to run. I realized that I had dropped my wand. I turned, and there was Reali, laughing, and waving it in her hand.

'Give it *back*!' I screamed, but she only waved it faster, and then, like an elephant, charged toward me. She pursued me through the gloomy midway, jiggling and laughing and shouting all kinds of obscenities, and the blackness bore down like death.

I awoke this morning bathed in sweat. The first thing I did was look for my wand, and found it safely packed in my case as always. I was so distressed from the dream that I bungled an elementary French Drop in my performance this morning. No-one noticed. If only I could dispose of dreams like that as easily as I slip coins into my *servante*. . . . Now as I write, the little trailer in the carnival that serves as my home seems smaller than a cupboard. If I don't get out I'll go quite mad.

Tony is bright, cynical, energetic... an excellent trilogy. He was working as a clean-up boy in the carnival until I hired him as my assistant. Now he's bound he's going to become a magician. I admire his audacity. 'I want to learn *everything*,' he told me the other day. 'You can't,' I answered. 'Even *I* don't know everything.' 'It's only a matter of time,' he argued, 'You're still young; why can't I learn everything you know?' I laughed at that. 'First of all, you'd be shocked to know my age and anyway I won't tell you. Second of all, you can't learn one iota of what I know. Third of all, the thing to know first of all is that you can know nothing. Learn that and we may get somewhere.'

'Come on, I've only got about ten years to catch up with you!' he cried.

'You've got ten eternities to catch up with me.'

'I want to be a magician, I want to have power over *them*!'

'Them,' I echoed.

'Them,' he replied.

'You want to lock people up in your movements, you want to map the dark side of the moon, you want to thrust yourself into the burning bush and burn your hands. . . .'

He didn't understand, so I put him to work on some elementary knots. After half an hour he was furious. 'How long do I have to practise *this*?' he groaned.

'Only about a year,' I answered. 'After that I'll show you the French Drop.'

'What the hell's the French *Drop*?'

'It's the technique of getting something out of one hand while you misdirect attention to the other.'

'Sounds like the title of a dirty book,' he mumbled. Then in a more serious mood he returned to the knots.

Now he sorts, cleans and repairs my apparatus every day. Last week I put him to work building a new set of props—a wooden wall braced with slanted beams at the back. I planned to use it only once. When the day arrived for my new performance the air was dark, indicating a summer storm. A crowd gathered around the wall, waiting. I appeared, removed my shoes to show that they weren't magnetized, and began to climb the wall. Horizontally. I stopped in the middle, my face turned to heaven, and watched the storm clouds gather. I was very comfortable; my blood sought a new level. People began to whisper. They waited for me to do something. Actually I was so comfortable I became slightly soporific. I put my hands in my pockets.

'He's putting his hands in his pockets,' someone said.

'He's bringing them out of his pockets. . . .'

I almost fell asleep, it was like lying on my back in bed. Suddenly the storm broke.

'Hey, you can't stand sideways like that, nobody can!' came an hysterical female voice.

'It's all done with mirrors,' said her escort.

I pulled a few rabbits out of my pockets.

'It's simple levitation,' someone said.

'It's not levitation because he's standing on his *feet*, *sideways*!' cried the woman.

The rabbits scurried up and down the wall.

'The rabbits are doing it *too*!' shrieked the woman.

'It's all done with mirrors,' came a voice. 'Besides that, the rabbits've all got magnetic feet, anyone can tell.'

'What about *him*, *he* hasn't got magnetic feet!'

Lightning came. I turned my head sideways and gazed at them. They looked like they were lying on top of one another. God, it was funny. I laughed some sideways laughter. The rain broke finally. Horizontal rain. I came down and all the people disappeared.

'How did you do it, how did you do it, how did you *do* it?' Tony pleaded.

'Mirrors.' I said, 'It's all done with mirrors.'

The manager told me that after my performance there was a record attendance in the Centrifugal Machine; everyone wanted to be revolved at high speed and glued to the bare walls like flies.

Now the summer is almost over. Tony and I pack up and return to the city. Vertically.

II

Tony pressed me for weeks afterward about the performance until I finally gave in and whispered in his ear, 'Akasa!'

'Akasa?'

'*Akasa*. An Indian word meaning levitation. Akasa can be achieved only by projecting a certain cerebral electricity that interrupts gravity. Negative electricity in fact.'

'O come on!' Tony cried.

I asked him if he had a better explanation. No, he hadn't.

I told him I had learned the trick in India a thousand years ago. Furious, he returned to his knots. 'If I could just read your mind—!' he complained.

'Read your own mind, Tony, then you will have read the world's mind. Then. . . .'

'O *come on*!'

Work is scarce this season; I have no bookings anywhere. I am scarcely able to record what in fact I have been doing these last weeks, but record it I must. I've been working as a night-watchman in a Power House. From midnight to dawn in the humming guts of Machine, myself a huge beating heart in the Power House, my pulse beating with a different rhythm than the pulse of Machine. I wander like Theseus through the throbbing maze of pipes and coils; I address myself to the generator politely, yet firmly, to the effect that one day it must acknowledge *me*. It intrigues, enrages me. This morning before leaving I put a hunch to the test. I asked a workman for the time, casually picking up his wrist between my fingers to see for myself. I had suspected it, now I knew. His pulse was geared to Machine. 'My watch runs a little fast,' he said. 'Subtract a quarter of an hour and you've got the right time.' I subtracted a quarter of eternity.

Why do I endure it? Because I am gorging myself; because I love and hate Machine. In magic I create worlds; my hands dance to their own rhythms. Here in the Power House there is another rhythm, another pulse. I begin to understand the anatomy of my enemy; I study the telepathy of its wires, its serpentine transforming coils. I listen to its heart; I hear the occult murmurs of magnetic poles as they swing and circle one another like antagonists who both love and hate. I charge myself on it, though its pulse will never dictate to mine, though its dance and mine will never be synchronized.

Now I sleep and dream by day, and I dreamed I stood at an intersection in the city. Six white roads led out from it like the legs of a great white spider. I looked around and wondered what name I should give the city, and finally I gave it the name of Julian. I whispered the name many times until the name recreated me and I began to grow up and out, larger and larger, until my left foot covered the whole of the intersection. The buildings became children's blocks beneath me; the clouds were miraculous white silks; the Lilliputians in their little cars fell away below me. I roared down to them, but my voice was inarticulate thunder. Thousands of red and white and blue dots formed immediately; I realized they were umbrellas. Then I thought that since I could no more speak to the people, I would perform for them. I took three clouds and knotted them together, but before I could complete my trick, the Lilliputians disappeared. I had merely created rain.

I put out my hand and clouded the sun—but wait—did I want to become a mere weather-god? Frustrated, I leaned over and picked up one of the Lilliputians and let him run around my palm awhile. Then I brought my eye down close to him to observe his activities. He had given up trying to escape and was now sitting in the long wadi of my life-line and scribbling something on a piece of paper. He sharpened his pencil to a needle-point and poked it into my iris. I winced in pain. Then he began writing something clear across my eyeball. I was going to go blind. I put him down again and blinked several times to get my sight back. I was intensely curious about the Writing on the Eye, but there was no mirror big enough for me in my present size to aid me in the reading of it.

Now I was growing even larger; I stepped out into the suburbs and from there into open country. Here was the place to perform. I rolled up my sleeves so that God could see I had nothing hidden in them. I ripped up a few hundred miles of railway track for a wand; I lifted layers of the multi-coloured countryside for my silks; I peeled highways from the earth for my ropes. I tied a yellow cornfield onto a highway and swung them round; I tied two small roads together and fastened a brown wheatfield securely between them. I uprooted three water towers and flattened them into coins. But my performance was interrupted once more, by the fact that my size continued to increase. My feet became conscious of the earth's curvature and I had trouble keeping my balance. Earth's atmosphere stopped at my waist; I slipped from the globe and stood in space. A few moments later the earth was the size of an orange, so I peeled it and heaved the peelings into infinity. Then I squeezed the blue juice of its seas into my mouth, carefully spitting out mountain ranges, submerged continents, continental shelves, polar ice caps and, finally, the long metallic axis, which I was delighted to find really did exist.

Nothing remained to do but juggle. So I juggled stars, in groups, in galaxies . . . and I wondered if there were anyone around to watch my performance. Close by me, through a milkwhite haze I could see the head of a tiny horse; it was lost in a bubbling sea of suns. I dipped my hand into the foam and picked it up and played with it awhile, but soon it too began to disappear until at last it was only a small grey puddle of quicksilver that vanished into the pores of my skin.

Now there was darkness; there was no more magic; there were no more galaxies. There was a mighty nothing that filled me with terror. The last thing I remember is peering into the utter reaches of the universe and seeing a shimmering silver form at the end. At the moment I realized it was *myself*, I awoke.

Last week I got into a conversation with one of the workmen. I told him every atom in his body was another universe. 'No kidding,' he said.

I tie and untie myself like Tony's sorry knots.

My fears are still as clean and primitive as the fears Adam had when he awoke to find himself alone in the awful garden of the world. I cannot bear for the light to go out, ever. I remember seeing an eclipse as a child in my last life, and the memory of it has never left me. The Dragon biting off the edge of the sun, consuming it bit by bit, and my hair on fire with fear. Perhaps it's because of this that I'm now trying to create a darkness that is not dark—a *black light*, in fact, a death that glows.

Today I showed Tony how to execute a French Drop. 'Look,' I said, 'you pass your hand over the egg, thus, and it appears to disappear, and you say to yourself *the egg is neither here nor there nor anywhere in particular, but like everything else in the universe its existence depends on your seeing it—that alone—and its existence is the gift of your inner eye.* But Tony interrupted me at that point crying, 'All's I want to know is how the hell do I move my *hands*!'

'O *that*,' I said, and proceeded to show him.

'There is darkness and there is light,' I said, gazing into the eyes of my audience and spinning a cardboard sun before them. Emerging from its spin it was black as night. 'Now there are many kinds of eclipses,' I went on. 'Eclipses of the sun, eclipses of the moon, eclipses of the mind. . . .'

The people shuffled their feet and coughed uncomfortably.

'And there are many kinds of light!' I said, and motioned for Tony to flick off all the electricity in the room. Then I lit a small torch and spoke through the flame. 'You will observe that the room is now dark and the torch is lit. Now, observe. . . .'

Tony switched the lights back on. I continued to hold the burning torch in my hand. 'The Lord's light is white,' I cried, 'but the lamps of the Devil are black!'

The torch darkened, but *still burned*, darkened to grey, to charcoal, to black.

Black fire, *black light*. The flames danced like deep jet shadows. The room and the people in it became a photograph in negative. I saw dark faces and white albino hair.

'Turn out the lights!'

'Turn *on* the lights!' they cried.

I was intoxicated. Inverted fire. Backwards Prometheus stealing the darkness from the gods.

Finally I snuffed the thing out and the photograph became positive. There was a hesitant scattering of applause. No-one congratulated me on my achievement. The eclipsed ones went home.

'Can *you* be eclipsed?' Tony asked me later.

'What do you mean?'

'Can *you* be tricked?'

'Never!' I laughed. 'Never!'

I'm starting to feel like a battery, my pulse charged by the Power House. Daily I live and die. I turn in on myself like a great hook and fish myself from my sleep to go and guard Machine.

A generator is what you put mechanical power into to make electrical power.

A motor is what you put electrical power into to make mechanical power.

A dynamo is a combination of the two. I am a dynamo, the Two-in-One, Divine Dualism, the Power and the House, the House and the Power, the Power and the Glory forever amen. I drift though the pale labyrinthine streets. What an affront it is to me that the city exists on its own terms. Sometimes, sadly, I bend down and pull bright cadmium scarves from between the cracks in the pavement. I give them to the children I meet.

Somehow I must relate to the city, let its chaos be my own. But no—I'm not going to be tricked into reality! I do a handstand and watch the people walking upside-down, their heads dipping down into the pale cobalt pool of the sky. A policeman tells me I am obstructing pedestrian traffic. I tell him it's my profession to obstruct pedestrian traffic. He is not amused.

The *language* of Machine. Rugged sensor and remote indicator signal butterfly valves. Cation resins and gasket-less cup-orifice unions. Stokers and cut grates, manifold valves and tilting discs. Toggle nozzles and flow nozzles. Finned heat transfer tubes. Spindle thrust. The shuttle activates hermetically sealed switch contacts. O flanged orifice!

I walk through the small streets, the secret parts of the city's anatomy. Dirty children perform strange rituals on the pavement all around me. Jacks and marbles, klackers, skipping ropes. *Step on a crack and you'll break your mother's back!*

Hey, it's the magician! Do a trick, mister, do a trick!' A boy tugs at my sleeve and I can't refuse. I tie a red handker-chief onto a white one; I toss them into the air; when I catch them they're striped like candy canes. In a moment they're real candy canes, and I break them into little pieces and pass the pieces round. All the dirty little faces smile. This is the pain of reality amid the marvelous.

I flourish my wand before them and a long stream of fluorescent ribbons flies in the wind. Small fingers grasp the ends of the flowing colours. I don't see their ragged clothes, I don't see the thinness of their bodies, I don't see the awful brightness of their eyes, I don't see the dying dreams that hover above them like ghosts, I don't see how small they are beside the city. I hide my wand beneath my cloak and for a moment I imagine it's a knife I plan to plunge into my guts. They keep calling for me to do another trick. Frightened, I throw my precious wand at their feet; they scream and jostle each other to reach it. Frightened still, I turn and run down a lane, then stand panting against a wall. Look, I have ripped my sceptre clean out of my flesh, I have given them my magic sceptre loaded with a sea of silks. They'll fight over it and eventually break it; they won't understand how to make it work. Ah, what does it matter?—it's only a lightweight pistol-shaped meter with revolving jaws; it's nothing but a catalytic fluid-cracking unit or a digital scanner, or a mere superheat feedwater sump pump. . . .

Ah, but they're breaking me in half down the lane!

Now I survey the city from my rooftop, and sometimes I let my hands dance over it as if I were conducting an eccentric symphony whose musicians are robots and whose instruments are a myriad machines. I am becoming strangely tired, but in my tiredness there is a nameless excitement, an impossible suspense. *Something is going to happen.* Tony still struggles with the French Drop, and I tell him the secret is not to let the right hand know what the left is doing (or vice versa) . . . and the ultimate secret is that the brain must be ignorant of what both are doing. He protests. I ask him if he has ever once seen me watching my own hands when I am performing. No, he says, he hasn't. That is because my hands have their own brains, I say, each of my fingertips possesses a brain. . . . He still protests.

The Power House must go, *that's* what's on my mind, that's what's been giving me the creeping sensation that's been with me for days. I'm still weak from my recent castration in the lane, but I have work to do. The Power House must go. I stumbled upon a children's science book recently and read that 'the human body is like a wonderful electrical generator that produces and transmits electricity, and the centre of this wonderful generator is the brain!' I read on, horrified and fascinated. 'Think of it, millions of tiny tiny electrical cells all over your body, isn't it wonderful, isn't the human body an amazing mechanism?'

I throw up my hands in despair over the city and the insane symphony stops. I am reaching a kind of Apocalypse; I know I am destined to end the world. I flex psychic and physical biceps for the task ahead. I'm going to crash the pulse of the Power House. It will be gone, destroyed, and I, Julian, will arise out of the electrical rubble unharmed and in fact renewed like the phoenix whose existence is a direct affront to time and death. *Whether I win or lose, I always win.* As if in answer to my thoughts, Tony switches off an electric light. I will go back on the roof for a while later in the night, and search the skies for the coming of the Horsemen.

Today I began. I cut off the telephone and threw it into the middle of the floor; I tore light bulbs out of their sockets and it was like plucking out the eyes of many Cyclopses; I severed wires with a meat knife; I yanked the motor of the refrigerator out of its box and added it to the heap on the floor; I trailed yards and yards of electrical entrails around the room; I attacked the stove, ripped out the wire coils of the burners and threw them onto the pile; I delicately removed the tubes of the radio as if performing an operation on adenoids. To the ever-growing junk-heap I added a few small magnets, several batteries, an alarm clock and Tony's wristwatch. Then I stomped on the pile and did a little jig until everything crunched together into one horrible metallic mass. I stood back and studied the electrical rubble, pleased, relieved. But I was tense as well, for time was running out, and I could feel grains of thin sand sliding down the hourglass of my body.

Today I put on my garments of motion, my cloak and my boots—the cloak that looks as if it is always at war with wind, the boots with wings at the heels that only I can see. I went out and walked through the streets, black and silver. The heels of the boots clicked against the pavement. People were anxiously watching the skies for a thunderstorm, but I was the thunder. City, O City, I murmured, whose psyche is a subway, whose forehead is a pavilion of asphalt and steel, I will conceal you in my sleeve, I will drop you into my *servante*.

Then there was thunder, the sky split, it was the first day of the world, the streets were slick and black. I stretched out my hands and began to repeat my own name softly, softly, *Julian, Julian*, as the rain fell softly down my arms, and the name became the answer to everything, the beginning and the end of me, genesis, apocalypse, life and death. *Julian, Julian*, and the name questioned and answered me, and it was every name that ever was and will be and it was the name of the thunder and the name of the city. The lightning was like a giant probing rod, an electrical wand. I wanted it and I was going to get it somehow; I was going to grab it and fling it across the city. Days, memories flew like electrons in orbit around my skull; I was Mesmer and Galvani and Zeus, I was positive and negative, doublepoled like the earth; I was wet with rain and yet I burned. Had I died then you could have pulled my skeleton apart and found every bone a wand. I was Julian, and I was man, I was all of you and none of you, I was in the beginning, I was dead and born.

I caught the lightning at last in my fist. I hurled it southeast toward the Power House. A great conflagration lit up the sky and fires of a hundred colours danced. Then it was all over; the fuses of the city spluttered and died and the lights went out forever.

There is no more time; I scribble this by candlelight and soon it will be dawn. I am inheriting myself minute by minute; I am moving into time which is not time, leaving behind me the broken machinery of the world, clocks, watches, artificial lights. I am possessing me, I am creating minutes and hours with the movements of an inner sun. The clock of the world is broken and I own myself at last. All the molecules of the world are a string of beads I toy with in my fingers. I will turn the stars of morning into sequins and sew them into my cloak. . . .

If you find this journal—(for I must leave it behind)— remember that the Master of Illusions doesn't make you believe what he wishes, but what you wish. Remember that all this was not my dream, but yours, that I speak from within you and you hear. And if you are laughing I am also laughing, and if you are weeping I am also weeping, and where this journal is, I am.

III

It seems he walked through many streets and knew many deaths before the dawn, and spoke to himself in circles and riddles. And when the light of morning came the children once again gathered round him singing and chanting and speaking in the ancient mysterious tongues only they remember.

'You're a tall man, you look like God,' one of them said.

'No, God is taller than that,' said another.

And one boy grabbed his cloak to get him to do a trick, but Julian cried, 'Don't touch me, don't hurt me!'

'I don't know my way home,' one girl said.

'Neither do I,' he answered. 'It's very far and very near.'

'I don't understand you,' said the girl.

'Yes you do, child,' he answered.

And the children followed Julian to the carnival grounds, playing and throwing balls on the way. It was about four in the afternoon. 'Winter is coming; we leave the sun,' Julian said.

The carnival was closed; there were a few empty booths and the big old ferris wheel and nothing else. The group climbed over the fence and entered the naked grounds of the carnival.

'I'm going on the ferris wheel,' Julian said.

'You can't, there isn't anybody to run it!' one of the children cried.

'Nevertheless I'm going. Watch me if you like.'

And the children stood in awe at the bottom and watched Julian get on.

'He's just pretending,' someone said.

The Wheel was rusty; its mechanism was tightly locked. Julian smiled faintly, the first smile in a long time.

'Look!' a child cried. 'The wheel's going round and no-one's turning it!'

The children watched in silence as the huge Wheel creaked and groaned in the empty carnival. It gained speed and became a circular blur.

And the laughter of Julian broke out from the Wheel, circular laughter. Once or twice the children caught a fleeting glimpse of him with his head thrown back and his hands outstretched. His cloak flew and his hair flew and he laughed and laughed.

The children waited in silence for a long time. Then slowly and painfully the Wheel ground to a halt and its machinery locked with a loud click.

They waited for the magician to come down. But the Wheel was empty and Julian was not upon it.

SNOW

She, of course, was used to it. Twenty-five years of parkas, furlined snowboots, mittens, scarves and crunching, slushing, sliding through it on the way to work or school. It was a Thing that covered the country four or five months a year, not unlike that billowy white corpuscle or whatever it was that went mad and smothered the villain of the film *Incredible Journey*. But for *him*, fresh from the Mediterranean, it was a kind of heavenly confetti, ambrosia or manna, and he rushed out half-mad at the first snowfall and lost himself in the sweet salt cold. He even dreamed of snow and he had a weird talent for predicting the next snowfall. He'd sleep and see tiny people coming down from the sky in parachutes that were snowflakes, a rain of infinitesimally small doves, ejaculations of white blossoms—the sperm of the great sleeping sky tree.

All through September and October his blood rose in anticipation of the cold, while all around him people lost their summer energy and grew weary and irritable as they thought of the long white siege ahead.

In December he trudged around frozen and delirious with joy in his soft Italian leather shoes with the pointed European toes, while she, bundled up to the chin with countless nameless pieces of wool and fur, hardly able to turn her head to see him, wondered how he could stand having to take his pants to the cleaner's twice a week to get the slush and wintry crud cleaned off of the cuffs. He made snowballs with his *bare hands*, if you can imagine, and when the tips of his ears turned a ghastly white from the cold, it never occurred to him to buy a hat. Coming indoors after an hour or two of strolling through a blizzard he would be *laughing* and freezing as if the winter were a great white clown someone had created solely for his amusement. She meanwhile, huddled in front of the oven or even the toaster, would try to unnerve him with horrendous tales of winter in Winnipeg. 'If you think *this* is something,' she would gasp, 'you should see what it's like out *west*!' and go on to describe how as a child she used to walk to school in the morning through shoulder-high snowbanks and by the time she got to the schoolyard there would be icicles in her nose and all round her mouth and her lips were so frozen she couldn't speak, and all the kids would be trying to laugh with their wooden lips. But he laughed too when he heard the story, and told her he wished he'd been with her out there, because, he explained, what thrilled him wasn't feeling the cold but letting the cold feel *him*.

Actually, she was quite a good sport with him that first winter he was in Kanada. At midnight after a heavy snowfall, they'd go into a little park where the swings and slides stood like skeletons in the blackness, and he, trembling with excitement, would put his foot into a fresh snowscape and examine the footprint of man marring the virgin whiteness. 'A giant step for mankind,' she'd say, as if the park were a moonscape, and slowly slowly they would walk forward pretending they were astronauts, clumsy and weightless in the midnight park, pouncing with glee on a swing or a slide or a water-fountain and radioing back to Earth that they had found evidence of an intelligent civilization. She would pick up a boulder—which turned out once to be somebody's frozen bowling shoe—and he, zooming in with his invisible

77

TV camera, would relay the image to the millions of viewers in Tokyo and New York and Paris and London and Montreal. Then they would take imaginary pictures of each other standing triumphantly in front of the swings, or gazing rapturously at a gleaming slide, which seemed to be giving off inter-galactic signals, like the rectangular slab in *Space Odyssey*.

For the first half hour or so she found it fun; they made cryptic triangles and squares in the snow and she even taught him how to make an 'angel' by lying on his back in the snow and swinging his arms up and down on both sides. But he was always wanting to prolong the excursions long after the cold had crept into her bones and she, wet through and shivering horribly, would have to wait for him to finish his angels—sometimes five, six, even seven of them all done in a neat circle around the water-fountain with their wings facing many points of the compass.

Gradually they became quite serious about what they should make of each fresh snowscape. They would stand on the brink of the park sometimes for five or ten whole minutes debating what they should inscribe there with their feet or hands, not wanting to waste the cleanness, the newness of the snow on trivial ventures. Moonscapes and angels started to pall on them, so one night they decided to do a series of gigantic initials, which seemed easy but was actually quite difficult because they had to make tremendous Nureyev-like leaps between the various strokes of the letters. When they still had some space left he decided to write his name, but he got all fouled up in the middle trying to do the splits between the bottom of an 'O' and the top of an 'R.' So he fell down flat in the middle of his name and got up protesting that it all came of not knowing how to write English well.

Another night they made a magic circle with segments bearing Cabbalistic Hebrew letters, and they both leapt into the centre of the circle and stood there under the stars and made secret wishes that are not our business to know.

Another night they were tired and spent the time throwing snowballs at tree trunks, which left hazy white circles like the fist-marks of avenging angels.

Another night they did Fantastic Footprints and Imaginary Beast tracks, trying to make the park look as if it has been the battleground between three-footed humans and hideous monsters who walked sideways like crabs. It took two hours to finish and though she had serious doubts as to whether it had been worth the effort, he was swollen with pride. You'd think he'd just completed a painting or a novel.

He was forever thinking up new things to be done with the snow. He considered (seriously) painting it, even flavouring it with sacks full of lime or lemon powder, and would have gone ahead with his plan had she not discouraged him by informing him you couldn't buy lime or lemon powder by the sack. So they made snowmen and snowwomen and snowchildren and snowanimals and snowstars. (A snowstar is a big ball of snow with long icicles—if you can find them—protruding out of the sides.) They made snowstars until her hands hurt. They made snow-trenches—where they lay in wait for the invisible army of abominable snowmen to come—until she thought she'd go mad, screaming mad. They made white fairy castles, they made white futuristic city-scapes, and they made footprints, footprints, footprints.

So I suppose what developed was, after all, to be expected. Which is not to say that she herself expected it in the least. When the night of the blizzard came and he hadn't showed up at his usual time, she got worried, very worried. And so she put on her fur-lined boots and her parka and her scarf and her mittens and went trudging out in the direction of the park. The snowfall that night was like a rapid descent of stars; they came down obliquely, razor-sharp, and her face stung and reddened and burned. *Snowfire*, she thought. Another word.

And she *was* surprised, though not totally, to find Grigori lying there at the bottom of the slide that gave off signals like the metal slab in *Space Odyssey*, with his Mediterranean hair all aflurry from the wind and his absolutely naked stone dead body wedged somehow into the snowdrift, and his arms outstretched at his sides as if he'd been making his last *angel*.

But what really got her was the smile on his face. He never did feel the cold.

NOMAN

PART 1
THE BOOK OF JUBELAS

Who killed Noman?

He stood there and died, just like that. And we were all with him, down there in the ravine, in pain.

I said: *I probably killed him with my homemade wine.*

Omphale said: *I miscarried him.*

Kali said nothing.

And Noman's body lay there in its brown trench-coat under a thin blanket of Kanadian snow, lay there with all its crazy wounds.

I said: *I didnt' kill him.*

Omphale said: *I didn't kill him.*

Kali said nothing.

One minute he was lighting a cigarette and the next minute he was dead. In the ravine, right in the middle of town, of all the stupid places. We had gone down to celebrate the Saturnal—(his idea)—and we took with us wine, and torches. At one point Kali threw back her black head and asked: 'What's a Saturnal, anyway—Noman, are you listening?'

(People always asked him if he was listening, and he always was.) And he crept up behind her and said, 'Why *this* is, of course!'

Which was a typical sort of answer coming from Noman. One minute he was lighting a cigarette and the next minute he was dead. Dead with a dozen crazy wounds. Dead with his brown hair upon the snow. He fell softly as a bird, bleeding in a dozen places at once.

Let me investigate this crime.

I want to get one thing straight right off the bat. These crazy names of ours were *his* idea. He said we should have names that told something about what we were like. My name for instance—Jubelas—reminded him of Rome and jubilees and things like that. Well he was halfway right. I do have some Italian in my background, but also a lot of Irish and a spot of French-Kanadian. I'm not so sure about the name he gave my wife—Omphale—because I found out that it has some connection with belly-button. Anyway, she certainly didn't seem to mind. That's the funny thing. Nobody ever *minded* Noman. Even when he wrecked your life. I used to live for real; I believed everything. Now nothing's real. Noman came from nowhere and went nowhere and fouled everything up for good.

It all started in mid-September. Omphale and I had decided we were going to save up to buy a farm and raise bees. We were on our way to meet Kali—a friendly character we'd known off and on for a few years. She always wore black, but she had 31 satin shirts, all different colours, one for every day of the month. One time we'd seen her she'd been threatening to pack up her bags and go to India for ever. We said Bon Voyage. But she couldn't decide which of her shirts to take, so she didn't go. Besides, she told us after that she couldn't leave the country because she didn't have a good enough photograph for a passport. Anyway, this is all beside the point. What I'm trying to say is that Omph and I were walking toward the restaurant and arguing about whether a bee-farm is an *apiary* or an *aviary*, when all of a sudden we stopped short and looked ahead.

He was standing there. Under a street-light, wearing a

brown trench-coat with the collar turned up. I could tell right away he was as foreign as they come; I mean, only foreigners know how to wear trench-coats like that. Like it was hanging on him, *alive.*

Neither of us knew why we stopped, so we looked at each other and started walking again, but as we passed him he said very softly, 'Hello, Jubelas.'

'Sorry, you've got the wrong man,' I told him, without looking back.

But then he stepped in front of us and looked me dead in the eye and smiled and said, 'Well who else are you, if you're not Jubelas?'

Now I gave that some thought and little by little it started to make sense. I don't really expect anybody to understand, though. And there's no way I can describe how it was he sort of fell into step beside us, just like that. He walked real funny, very soft and careful like he was treading barefoot on broken glass. And somehow he made us feel like we were accompanying *him*, not the other way around.

We got to the restaurant and went in. Kali was sitting waiting for us at a booth at the back. She had two suitcases with her so I could tell she was threatening to take off for India again. Or maybe Port Hope, where she owned a small sailboat. We sat down and I felt awkward because, not knowing his name, I couldn't introduce the stranger to her. I started to order coffees, but he broke in and did it himself. Like he was taking over.

Then we all sat there going Stir Stir with the spoons until I finally leaned over and asked him politely what his name was.

'Oh, I'm sorry,' he said, turning and looking at me with those eyes. 'I *didn't* introduce myself, did I? *Noman is my name, and Noman they call me, my father and my mother and all my fellows.*'

And that was that.

I mean, the way he said it made you sit up and think, *well of course*. Like the name explained everything. We all relaxed then and started talking. He spoke strangely. It wasn't as if he had an accent, exactly . . . it was more as if he was speaking in *italics*, if you know what I mean. I got to feeling so friendly that once I gave him a big friendly whack across the shoulders. Stupidest thing I ever did. He wasn't the sort of guy you whacked over the shoulders. So I sat there and stared at his trench-coat. Like I'd hurt the *coat*, you know?

Omphale, I could tell, was off in another world, listening to the stranger. I wasn't sure what was wrong with her, but I wasn't jealous, or anything, because she was a good fifteen years older than him. And it was obvious that Kali had forgotten all about India and Port Hope. She sat there with a funny smile on her mouth, her black dress growing blacker.

I interrupted them once and asked Noman to say *Traw-nah* for me. But he didn't say it right. He said it *Toronto* with all the t's. Then I asked him to say *Canada* and he said *Kanada*.

'Hey, what country do you come from, Noman?' I said. 'No kidding. What country?'

But he didn't answer. Anyway I had it all figured out. He had to be pure Spanish. Castilian. He was so *interested* in everything that was going on around him. That proved he was foreign, all right, but I figured he had to be part of some lost Spanish aristocracy, what with the dark skin and the trenchcoat and the way he lit cigarettes. You have to be idle and rich and foreign to get so absorbed in things.

So I asked him, casually. 'Hey, Noman! Hace frio¿ no es verdad?'

But he just looked at me for a minute and then smiled like I was out of my mind. I remember wondering how come he didn't take his coat off inside. He loosened it in front, to give it a rest, and sat back with one hand in the pocket and the other holding coffee and cigarette. With anyone else that would look sloppy—but that's what I mean about being foreign; you can do those things. No matter what position he was in he was always graceful—a real powerful kind of grace, the kind you find in blacks and rich Spaniards and Russian dancers. It's because all the power is held back.

'Have you ever noticed how many letters we drop in English?' he was saying, '... leaving so many silent consonants and unspoken sounds?'

I told him I'd never given it much thought.

'... and how by night,' he went on, 'we send out for Chinese and Italian food, which we never eat by day?'

I confessed I hadn't thought about that either.

'Italian pizzas in the midnights of Kanada. Chow Mein and Sweet and Sours in the small hours of the morning. By day it's mashed potatoes, white bread, cornflakes. ...'

I told him I didn't get the point. But he didn't seem to hear me. 'Kanada,' he sighed. 'Paper-maker. Like a great blank sheet in the world's diary. Who'll make the first entry?'

And just then Kali broke in. 'Foxes,' she said. 'Foxes leaving dark marks in the snow.'

I could see the conversation was getting way out of hand, so I broke in with what I thought (and still think) was a terrific joke.

'Hey, Noman!' I said. 'What comes into town wearing a dirty white sheet and riding on a pig?'

He raised his eyebrows in anticipation. I allowed a reasonable amount of time to pass.

'*Lawrence of Newfoundland!*'

But Noman was not amused.

(How can I describe him so you'll understand? First of all, he wasn't *bad*. He never lied, for instance—he just talked truth like it was a different kind. And he kind of pounced on you like a lion and ate you up ... but very polite about it, very gentle. When he looked at you, his eyes were full of surprise, as if he never asked or expected to see the things he saw. Everything sort of played itself out before him. He himself *did* nothing, but he made it all happen).

When he left that night, he gave me his phone number— (in fact he gave *everybody* his phone number)—and honest to God, I didn't have the slightest intention of calling him up. But every time I changed my trousers during the next week the phone number would keep falling out and reminding me, so I finally did call him. (*Who*, I ask you, would bother with such a nut except another one?) He seemed pleased to hear from me—but then, that funny whispery voice of his, you could read it however you wanted—and we went for a walk downtown. We passed a bible-thumper outside one of the big department stores, who kept shouting *I am Alpha and Omega*! Noman seemed to know who Alpha and Omega were which is how I came to abandon my first theory that Noman was Castilian, and decided once and for all he had to be Greek. But do Greeks wear trench-coats? I asked myself. I was getting mixed up. I did check his shoes, though, and they looked Greek enough. Anyway, to make a long story short, Noman walked up to the guy with the bible and asked him straight out if he was really Alpha and Omega. He said nicely enough that he *himself* wasn't, but that Christ was. Then Noman asked him what *that* meant, and the guy said,

'Are you questioning the word of God, my son?'

'No' (said Noman), 'I just want to know what the word *is*.'

'The word' (the guy went on), 'is Alpha and Omega.' Then he paused as if he just remembered something. 'And I am Alpha and Omega.'

'Well, I'm the whole alphabet,' said Noman, leaning

back against one of Eaton's plate-glass windows. 'Will you let me stand beside you and say I am *Alpha and Omega?*'

'No. You are a charlatan, young man. Besides, this is my corner.'

Noman got very sad after that, so we went into the first club we could find and sat for an hour glaring at each other over a bottle of liebfraumilch. I know how to say *How Do You Do* and comment on the weather in 23 different languages, so to test my Greek theory on him, I said, *Hey, Noman! Τι Κάνις, Καλά?* But he just looked at me with those brown eyes and I knew I'd struck out again.

After about twenty minutes we were both pretty far gone. We were into our second bottle of wine (mavrodaphne this time), and Noman asked the waiter to bring us over a telephone book. Then he started flipping through it and jotting down names and numbers. I asked him what he was doing, but he didn't answer until he was finished. Then he stuck the list in my face and leaned back and sighed and said, 'Look, Jubelas, look at the names!'

'The angel Lucifer,' I read, 'Angelo Lucifori.'

'Spiro Ikari,' he went on. 'Icarus. I'm going to phone them all, I'm going to find out if they *are* what their names are.'

I was pretty dubious. But we finally managed to get over to the telephone, and Noman started calling all the names on the list. It turned out the angel Lucifer owned one leetle vegetable store. Noman told him he was making an inquiry for the Council on the Study of Ethnic Peculiarities. Angelo said, *what do you want, I pay my taxes.* The next name on the list was Spiro Ikari. Noman announced, 'Spiro Ikari will be a second-generation Greek. He lives alone, writing outstanding aeronautic papers. Detached, brilliant, he's now proving the complete instability of the jumbo jet.'

'You're wrong,' I said. 'Spiro Ikari flips french fries in a restaurant.'

Noman phoned him and I'm damned if he wasn't a short-order cook.

We were left with John Incognito.

'John Incognito,' Noman announced. 'Is an ex-spy. He now works for a textile manufacturer who specializes in dark velvet curtains and theatre backdrops.'

'Wrong again,' I told him. 'John Incognito owns an advertising agency.'

We never did phone John Incognito. Maybe because we ran out of dimes, maybe because we didn't want to know.

Funny things started happening to me after I knew Noman. I got to feeling half nuts and nervous all the time. There's this story about a beautiful centipede who walked perfectly with all his legs, until somebody asked him which leg he moved first. He'd never thought about it before, so he forgot, and never walked again. Just stood there, trying to remember which leg came first. I mean, Noman made me *think*. I've never felt comfortable thinking. And I was always asking myself *who is he, what does he want, where does he come from*? What made it worse was that I was really attached to him. He could have been my own son, he gave me that feeling. But he never *told* me about himself, whether he had a family, things like that. It's always the same. With everything. When you *don't know*, you're interested.

He had an apartment up in the north end of the city; it was a small place with a big curved window that made it look like the wheelhouse of a ship. It was full of little statues made out of clay and stone and rusty metal. I never liked them; they made me feel as if I was sitting in a theatre. Whenever I visited him he'd stand by the window swirling a glass of brandy, and at any minute I'd expect him to take the wheel and steer the whole apartment with its passengers out over the skyscrapers of the city. At home he always wore a dark maroon thing, a lounge jacket, that made him look different. I could talk to it easier than I could to the trench-coat. He'd creep around in the maroon thing looking for cigarettes, and when he got interested in something he was saying, he'd light the filter end of his cigarette, and then go on as if nothing had happened.

He was so damned debonair. He sort of *leaned* into the world, testing the ground with his feet as if there was a big hole somewhere but he knew he'd never fall into it. I would have liked to be like that. I always felt so clumsy and Kanadian. Like the little tugboat that used to run to the island in winter with the sign inside that said it was only qualified to navigate in Minor Waters.

I hated it when the bunch of us went out together—me and Omph and Kali and Noman. I lost him then; everybody claimed him. Once I got so mad I went berserk. We'd been driving around all afternoon, and finally stopped in a restaurant off the highway. Omph ordered a large milk—(she never drank milk before)—and I sat there getting madder and madder. Finally I smashed the table with one hand and sent a spoon flying into the air, the way you jump a guy off a trampoline. I wanted to shout, but I just sat there with my mouth hanging open because I didn't know what to shout about. I'm frantically looking around for some excuse to blow up. Finally I find it. The juke-box, the Jesus juke-box. I stomp over to the thing and it's sitting there grinning and going Thump Thumpety-Thump with the disc whirling around inside its head. I start pounding my fists into the little buttons on the panel. I pound and pound until I hear something breaking. I stand back and roll up my sleeve and scream 'Don't stop me, anybody! This is my moment of glory!' And then I take the juke-box in my arms and bash it up and down and rattle it and shake it and kick it until it's dead. I'm standing there all finished now and the thing's going Grind Grind.

The owner screamed, 'You'll pay for this!' and ran for a phone. Noman got up and walked over to the counter, slow and calm. I saw him take out a cheque-book and write a cheque. Then he pulled out his wallet and it was full of identity cards. I never in my life saw so many identity cards —you could have played poker with them—and flashed them in the guy's face. Don't ask me what happened then. All I remember is the owner putting down the phone and taking the cheque and disappearing into the kitchen.

Then we all piled back into the car. I kept mumbling *I didn't mean to do it, I didn't mean to do it*, like a kid. And when nobody said anything I said, *why doesn't anybody say anything?* And Noman said nothing. *You never go nuts, do you*, I muttered under my breath. *You're nuts.*

Things started looking different to me . . . objects and buildings and people. Signs I'd never noticed before started screaming down at me from billboards. Mysterious things started happening in the subway. Noman couldn't explain it because, well, *he was making it happen* . . . does that make sense? Oh, I *told* him I thought I was going nuts, and he played with the rim of his brandy glass and made a high shrill sound with his fingertips.

'You're not going nuts, Jube, you're going sane,' he said. 'I know, it's hard to tell the difference.'

'Let's *do* something!' I said. 'Let's rob a bank, or go see a film, or something!'

'I hate films,' he said. 'The vast *fiction* of Rome unfolding before my very eyes. A Swedish camera exploring the pores on somebody's thigh. An American camera exploring miles of the lush blood-soaked vegetation of Asia. I hate watching people crawling out of a cinema after escaping 'reality,' then wandering through the seething streets looking for some excitement. Ugh. Wondering why Bloor Street can't be the Champs D'Elysée.'

Christ, I thought, now I couldn't even enjoy a good film

anymore. 'O come on!' I cried. 'You're fouling everything up for me!'

'If Noman is hurting you then there's no-one hurting you after all,' he said. 'If Noman is blinding you, then you aren't blind.'

Several weeks passed and I got to noticing small things, queer things, like how come he stayed so slim and athletic when the only exercise he seemed to get was walking around the apartment looking for cigarettes and touching all the little statues. I asked him what he did for a living and he said Nothing At Present, but when I pressed him about it he confessed he used to be a dancer.

'Dance for me, Noman!' I cried.

'No.'

'What's wrong—afraid you can't start?' I said.

'No,' he said. 'Afraid I can't stop.'

I asked him if he needed prompting, but he said he needed me to *dare* him, which I did. Then I asked him what kind of dancing he did, and he said there's only one kind. That went over my head, but I said I didn't mind what kind it was as long as it wasn't ballet. I can't stand ballet. Well, he put on a record, and it was some wild Russian song. I clapped my hands and he laughed out loud; I'd never heard him laugh like that before. Then he kicked his heels down hard on the floor, and he danced, o man, did he dance! He laughed and sweated and his hair went flying all over his face, and I could see hordes of drunk Cossacks burning and looting villages. The little statues shook like they were scared; I was afraid when I stopped clapping they would all drop dead. And Noman was all muscle and nerve; he had all kinds of energy stored up, waiting. We got around to the chorus for the seventh time and my hands were getting red and tired, but he kept on dancing, throwing little bits of himself all over the room, if you know what I mean. Finally he did stop, and collapsed into a chair and laughed and laughed, but I could still see a shadow of him twirling and falling on the other side of the room.

I had it all figured out. Noman was a Red. That's how come he never told anybody where he came from. Because he was an *ex*-Red. Defected, probably, like that Nureyev nut. Now he was lying low in Trawnah. That explained everything. Me, I'm broad-minded. I couldn't have cared less if he was Red. Russians, Jesus, they've got damn fine music.

So when I got home that night I said to Omphale, 'Omphale, guess what? Noman's Russian.'

'No, he's not,' she said. 'I already asked him, and he said No. But I got it all figured out. He's Albanian. Either that, or he's Circassian Arab. Tomorrow I'm going to learn from you how to say How Do You Do in Arabic. That'll put him on the spot. Remember in the film how Lawrence passed for a Circassian Arab when he was captured by the Bey . . .?'

'Which reminds me,' I said, 'of this terrific joke. What comes riding—'

'Jube,' said Omphale, 'I've *heard* that one.'

There was an early snow in the Laurentians that year, and we all packed into Kali's little car and headed for Quebec. Noman still wore his trench-coat. *Skiing*, for God's sake. We all stood at the top of a fairly steep slope, and everyone wanted to be the one to teach him how to ski. It was as if—I don't know—as if we were all afraid the snow would swallow him up, or that he'd go blind from the whiteness. As if the long cold slope threatened only him. Anyway, we decided Omph and I would go first, he would follow up and Kali would come last. Off we went, slowly at first, then the slope got steeper. I managed to look back once or twice to see how he was doing, and all I saw was a blurry cloud that seemed to be doing OK. Once, though, I had to make a sharp turn to avoid plowing into a tree, and I thought, Christ, he'll never make it. I swirled to a stop; so did the others, and we stood there peering back up the slope. He'd disappeared. Nothing.

'Noman, Noman!' I yelled, but there was no answer. Kali came gliding down to us in her black skis, cursing. Maybe he's dead, I thought. Funny what a weird thrill that gave me.

'Noman, Noman!' I yelled but my voice slid off into the wind, the snow. Nothing out there but a big pile of white. Somewhere high above us Noman lay calm and aloof, colder then the landscape. I started to get scared because now I was sure he was dead or dying out there in the white nothing—him who danced so well—and I started back up the trail to find him. I resented it when the others joined me. I mean, what business was it of theirs if Noman was dying?

Suddenly there was a movement ahead of me and a hand came popping out from under a big snowdrift.

'You dead, Noman, you dead?' I asked, clearing the snow away.

'I'm not dead, Jube,' he said.

'You're *not* dead?' I said, slipping and puffing and falling to my knees to feel him all over for broken bones.

'I'm not dead,' he said again. 'I'm not even hurt. My coat's been bruised, though.' and he felt all over the coat for wounds.

Then everyone else piled in, asking if he was dead and feeling around.

When we drove away that evening I was really depressed. Sort of deflated. Not that I wanted to find him *dead*, but I had this fantasy that if I had found him dead there in the snow, I would have lifted him up and carried him back up the long white trail and buried him under a pioneer log cabin and played Kalinka on the mouth-organ for his funeral.

I got to wandering around alone—something I'd never done before—and one day I got caught downtown in the middle of a big parade. Big phony floats came sailing past me, and everyone was screaming and pushing and I heard drums. I wanted to scream or kill somebody and the music went Blah de Blah. I felt as if my skull was going to split open like a ripe cantaloupe. Then down the road floats this huge gold float in the shape of a lion, a big papier mâché lion. Somehow I felt that it was coming after *me*, that it was going to bear down on me. And I was alone, more alone than I'd ever been in my life; big scared tears started streaming down my face. I smelled sweat and beer and corned beef all around me. And suddenly—I didn't know what I was doing—I ran out into the middle of the road screaming *Noman, Noman*! and everybody was laughing and yelling at me, and I didn't care. Then two cops came charging out of the crowd and told me I was obstructing the parade, but I tried to throw them off, shouting, 'Leave me alone, I gotta follow the gold lion!' By the time they got me back to the curb the big beautiful beast was far away. I knew from here on in I was alone.

I went into the nearest bookstore and made off with two books stuffed under my jacket—*Winnie the Pooh* in Russian and Trudeau's *Federalism*. I knew I'd never read them but I got such a charge out of stealing them that I wasn't satisfied. So I went into another store, and another, and looted like a mad pirate. I figured I could go on all day, stealing and stealing; I figured I had an undiscovered talent for it, because nobody caught me. Or maybe when you don't care whether you get caught or not nobody notices you. Being reckless put me above suspicion, and the more reckless I got the better I could do it.

Pretty soon I was loaded down with junk, and I bought a shopping bag to carry it all in. None of it was stuff that I wanted or needed, but that made it all the more fun. I had altogether:

two books, one wallet, three typewriter ribbons, two combs, a pipe, a white shirt, a pair of sandals, one screwdriver, a flashlight, two tubes of oil paint, one *Time* magazine, one *Modern Screen*, a gadget for squeezing orange juice and a pair of socks.

And I kept going over the list in my head because it distracted me from all the problems I suddenly had that I couldn't solve because I couldn't name.

One pair of socks, one *Modern Screen*, a gadget for squeezing orange juice, a white shirt, a flashlight. . . .

And I kept going over the list in my mind because it stopped me from seeing things I didn't want to see, things I never saw before I knew Noman. Like the woman who passed me once in the street with an open purseful of children's toy money. Like the big gold lion who for me was real.

Three typewriter ribbons, one *Time* magazine, a screwdriver, a gadget for squeezing orange juice. . . .

Because it made me forget how I was screaming inside. It made me stop thinking.

One pair of socks, a white shirt, three typewriter ribbons
and a   tri

     par   idge   pear

           in   tree.

        a

Omph was in pretty bad shape those days too, and she kept telling me about how she dreamed she had given miraculous birth to Noman in the middle of Bay Street after stars and planets had rolled around in her belly. And the newborn Noman, in the dream, was fully grown, wearing a Roman toga with a big gold buckle. He was impatient, and he stamped his foot, and he asked permission to leave. And Omph had cried out—'Leave? What do you mean leave? You've just been born! Babies don't leave!'

Now Omph wished she was a Roman lady leaning against milky white columns with bands of dark gold on her arms. She wanted to hear zithers—whatever they are—and hold big goblets in her hands full of dark sweet wine from Italy. She wanted to wander across mosaic floors wearing soft-thonged sandals, and out onto the terraces, being intelligent and patrician, and god knows what else. 'But Jube, it'll never be!' she cried once into my shoulder. 'I'm full of hollow places and holes. I'm not pretty. I hate all my clothes!'

Poor Omph. She would have liked to have a son like Noman, with strange broad feet and the roots of his teeth as strong as horses'. Once when Noman was in bed five days suffering from an abcessed molar, she persuaded him to go to a Latvian dentist to have it out. The same night she couldn't sleep; she got up and got dressed and took a cab to Noman's apartment, and slipped a shiny brand-new quarter under his door. Noman never mentioned finding the quarter, but he did show me the tooth. Enormous—like something out of the jawbone Samson fought with. Foreigners have such damn fine teeth. Omph practised saying '*Keef haalak?*' for a whole day once, then confronted him with it. But there was no response. She still insisted he was Circassian, though.

I told Noman for the thousandth time that I thought we were all going nuts. But he just smiled. I told him I felt like an animal, a savage in the city, and couldn't wait until me and Omph sold everything and went to the country to raise bees. Then he said a funny thing; he said *he* was the savage here. *Him*, with his trench-coat and brandy. *Him* with his statues and books with titles I couldn't even read. (*Wittgenstein's Tractatus*, for God's sake, what was that, some kind of foreign cook-book?) Then he said another funny thing; he said, *wait, let's have a Saturnal!*

'And what,' I asked, 'is a Saturnal?' thinking it was some kind of knockout cocktail he was going to fix us up.

'An ancient Roman festival,' he answered. 'They used to have it on the 17th of December. Like a Bacchanale, only different. Listen, we'll all go down into the ravine,' he went on, getting excited, 'with wine and torches. Possibly chocolate bars. Or bread.'

Jesus, I thought, can you beat that? Why didn't I see it before? Noman was Italian. A real Wop, just like me.

It was freezing on the 17th of December. My circulation wasn't circulating and my hands and feet were ice. There was no snow yet in the city but the ground was hard and dry. It was the week before Christmas, and the air had that feel about it, that tension. I didn't feel very festive; I was in the midst of tragedy. Everyone else looked pretty grim too, sort of anemic and pale as if they had chalk on their faces, or masks. We started down the trail into the ravine in the middle of town. I went first because I was carrying the main torch, not to mention the big jug of homemade wine, which I heaved back and forth, partly to keep my arm warm and partly to look like I was happy. Down we went, under the viaduct—(more people have jumped off of that viaduct . . .)—single file, deeper and deeper into the trails. I started to sing and I sang louder and louder because I felt so scared and cold. Suddenly somebody stopped and said, 'Let's find Saturn!' and we all looked up into the dark sky.

'It's the first on your right, past the big bluish star,' Noman said. Then I think it was Kali who said, 'Noman, you can't speak of *right* and *left* in astronomy!' And he answered 'It all depends on where you stand.' I remember thinking that Saturn didn't look like much after all, not enough to rate a whole ancient festival anyway. It was sort of sick looking for a planet, jaundice yellow in fact.

Then we were on the dark green floor of the ravine and the city's traffic was far away. We reached a clearing and I put my torch and wine-jar at the bottom of a tree, then scrambled up the tree, I guess to get away from everything. Omph sat down leaning against the tree trunk, and so did Kali, who had a closed white umbrella like a unicorn's horn in her lap. Noman stood alone in the middle of the clearing.

It was too quiet, 'Let's get this Saturnal off the ground!' I cried, but my voice sounded strange in the stillness. Kali meanwhile was mumbling, reading poetry or something, and out of the corner of my eyes I watched you, Noman, and you stood there getting ready to light a cigarette, holding the fire in your hands, your fingers cupped protectively around the flame. You were still and stony like one of your statues, as if you'd forgotten where we were, in the middle of a ravine in mid-December, celebrating a festival a million years old. After all, it was your idea.

Finally I couldn't stand the quiet any longer and I yelled down through the blackness, 'Hey, Noman, let's get this show on the *road*!'

And then you dropped dead.

I mean your knees folded under and you dropped. Dead. Just like that.

I got down from the tree and ran over to you and said, 'Noman?' What are you doing, Noman, lying there like that? With your hair all over the ground, with your brown trench-coat on?'

But you were lying face down and your coat was dead and everything was dead.

I figured I killed you. I figured it was the wine. I never was much good at making wine.

Then I saw how Omph was holding her stomach as if

she'd miscarried. Kali was clutching her shoulder, and for some reason I was grasping my knee in pain.

Then it started to snow, the first snow of the year, the weirdest spookiest snow I've ever seen, coming down in big sticky flakes, floating down, covering you.

I went nuts. But it wasn't so bad. I went quietly.

Then I saw red marks coming on your neck and hands. A thin stream of red was moving into the snow like a wiggly line of ink, writing something. I thought it might be a code, and I tried to read it, but it was a mad scribble. I expected to see angels come down from heaven to lift you away, but none came, and we all stood around white and numb and clutching ourselves.

And when I looked up into the sky I couldn't see Saturn anymore because the snow was too thick. It was like all the stars and planets were falling into my face. Like the universe was crumbling into sugar and sprinkling on your body.

Now I'm through writing all this down. I finished my investigation but I didn't solve the crime. Anyway, I don't believe your death. It's fiction, and it's evil, the way all fiction is evil. I think you escaped to some forest somewhere, you mad Circassian, to hunt foxes, to follow the dark marks they leave in the snow.

I'll stand in the middle of the ravine and howl like a big papier mâché lion. I'll howl your name until my lungs crack, like it was the city's name, like it was my name—and they'll come and whisk me away to the funny farm or the aviary or the apiary or whatever. Anything'll be better than this city of statues. I feel like a foreigner who doesn't speak the right language. Or maybe everybody else is speaking the wrong language. *Hace frio¿ no es verdad?*

Listen, Noman, wherever you are—I still got this big jug of wine left over from the Saturnal. It's almost spring now, and the snow is melting and the air is getting warm.

We'll take the jug, you and me, and go out into the country somewhere and lie on the grass and swill the stuff away for hours. We'll laugh and slap each other's backs like natural men, and I'll teach you how to say How Do You Do and comment on the weather in 23 different languages. And maybe you'll tell me that you played a fool trick and aren't dead at all . . .? Wow, we'll laugh at that, and drunk as lords we'll sing and stagger all over the fields full of bees, the green fields, under the yellow laughter of the sun, over the rivers and streams and through the big arch that leads into the forest. . . .

PART 2
THE BOOK OF KALI

I won't start off with a description of Noman, though I was the one who saw him coming out of the freezing lake with water dripping from him like quicksilver. Rather I shall begin with myself who am colubrine, and who he named Kali. (*Kundalini*, he said once, as if I lay coiled like the magic serpent at the base of his spine.) I haven't shaved my armpits for eight and a half years and at full moon I go stark mad. At the age of eight, an angel invaded my bed and showed me a terrible premature salvation. At the age of ten I was deflowered by a tree. My face is composed of precise planes and my eyebrows angulate (angulate?) to wide inverted V's and taper off toward the temples—(the *churches*, Noman, beating in my head). I have sensitive nostrils, like a colt's. My mouth hurts me.

I get bored easily (or at least I *did*), which was why I was continually making plans for India. Jube's already said that I never actually went, but then, a thought can be just as potent as a reality. Nowadays when I get bored (which is almost never) I mentally list a few images or incidents to stir my blood back into being, such as:

The existence of the Loch-Ness monster.
The burning of the Alexandrian libraries.
The biblical plagues.
Goya's *Rain of Bulls*.

The meaning of Noman.

All of which should explain quite clearly how it was I came to be standing downtown one day in late summer watching Noman demolish an old bank. Not *alone*, of course, he was with a crew of men employed by the Apocalyptic Demolition Co., and they were attacking one wall, pulling out cables and wires viciously, smashing away at the bricks. Noman was dressed in white, like an avenging angel, and as I watched, he bent over a red joint in the metal framework of the wall and attacked it with a torch. Loud flames issued from his fingers. I knew then I was lost. So I came back day after day to the site until he noticed me and came over to the wire fence and asked, '*What your name is?*'

'What do you *want* it to be?' I asked.

And he looked at me a long time with his head cocked to one side and said, 'Kali.'

'Then I am Kali,' I said. 'And you?'

He looked up to the skeleton of the bank, then higher up to where the skyscrapers lived, and said, 'I don't know. I have—how you say—amne *see*ah.'

'Then I'll call you Noman,' I said.

We began to meet regularly after that, mostly in restaurants, and I would try to help him improve his English. *The pen is, was and will be on the table. It would be on the table, but there is no table. It has been on the table since yesterday and will have been there two days when we come tomorrow.* Then he would take my hair in his hands and look at me long over the cold coffee cups and whisper, 'Yes Kali, the pen is on the table. Always.'

Or touch my forehead on both sides with his fingers and tell me he could hear the blood pounding in my churches.

Or explain how he had almost total amnesia and couldn't remember a thing about his past.

How could I have known it was all an elaborate act? I

believed his language problems were real. Small things seemed to prove it—like the day at my place when he ripped a milk carton to shreds because he couldn't read the instructions: OPEN HERE. It's hard to fake something like that.

But alas, I finally learned the awful truth.

Noman was Kanadian.

I found out the day we went swimming, and he came out of the dark water with drops of it falling from his arms and thighs like mercury. He shivered and sat down on the beach beside me and said, 'Kali, I am so many people.'

And I, not really listening because the sun was so warm and the sky so far, said, 'Figuratively, of course.'

'No, literally.'

We lay on our backs and listened to the sibilant waves telling the beach to go away. The lake regurgitated a turtle almost at our feet. Then the waves began to stutter; it was getting late. In the city there were great piles of coal and scrap iron, which glinted like giant scarabs in the sun. Cranes rose and fell like lazy giraffes. Close by us, on the shoreline, plastic things floated in the shallows like strange uncatalogued fish. A thundercloud passed over the cranes, the waves. I got up to leave.

Suddenly Noman said, 'Kali, I want to meet those two friends of yours, the ones who are going to raise bees.'

And I, still drowsy from the sun said, 'Why?'

'To prove something.'

'What disturbing thing do you want to prove?' I laughed. 'That the shortest distance between points is not a straight line?'

He smiled and handed me my bag. 'It just so happens, Kali, that there is a set of conditions under which the shortest distance is a *curved* line.'

'Good God!' I exclaimed. 'What are the conditions?'

'A revolving circumference. Something like that.'

'Incredible,' I said, putting on my sandals.

'Let's arrange a meeting,' he went on. 'But let's pretend you don't know me, OK?'

'OK,' I said.

Just then a black freighter passed us out on the lake and sounded some kind of signal. I stood there, mesmerized.

'Noman! Your English—it's *perfect*!'

'Why not?' he asked. 'It's my mother tongue.'

'You mean I sweated over those damned conjugations for nothing! What a dirty trick!'

'Forgive me,' he said. 'I just wanted to learn it all over again.'

'Monster!' I screamed. 'You mean you're *Kanadian*!'

I nagged him all the way back to my place, where, by the way, I had intended to cook up a storm of ethnic dishes, just for him. My fridge was stuffed with insane food, vegetables mostly, things like Dandelion Greens and Dried Fava Beans and Hearts of Artichokes. I'd even bought new books, *Cook your Way through Europe* and *The Yellow Quest: A Study of Indian Curry*. I was furious. When we finally got back I threw a can of pork and beans into a saucepan and glared at him over the table. He lit a cigarette and glared at me.

Then we laughed.

We staged our little rendezvous with Jubelas and Omphale. I was merely an observer, but like all good observers I was more involved than the observed. I couldn't quite decide which role I was supposed to play; I felt as if I were in a theatre where they were playing *Oh Kanada* and I couldn't decide whether to sit or stand, until I finally fell back from the exhaustion of indecision and did absolutely nothing. I watched Noman's strange game with Omphale and Jubelas, I watched it for weeks, months. Perhaps I was too close to it and didn't read it correctly. An ant, walking across a printed page can't read the words.

Anyway, I sat amid the chaos, with Jube saying How Do You Do in 23 different tongues, and thought—This Too Shall Pass.

Noman *became* whatever he encountered. He was snow, reflecting light. He was a vista. I used to sip Bloody Marys and smile blackly at Omphale, haunted by dreams of virgin births on Bay Street, or at Jube, turned hairy and antediluvian and afraid. Both of them imagining every sort of conceivable birthplace for Noman. He was Castilian or Circassian, he was Hungarian or Tangerian, he was one of the Rôm. Imagining a thousand possible tongues for him, for somehow it was incongruous that he could have worn so beautiful a coat, or danced so well in Kanada.

He was born in the year of our Lord 1940. Perhaps a star went nova over the Exhibition Grounds that day, perhaps not. Perhaps there was chaos on the Stock Exchange, perhaps not. Perhaps no-one has heard of Noman. He was tall and dark—(can you imagine him short and blond?)—and he had a birthmark on his inner thigh that looked like the great spiral nebula in Andromeda. In fact he still does, for he's not dead, but I'll get into that later. Someone else may say it looks like an egg, but Noman's inner thigh is none of their business. He has a small scar from a minor operation on his stomach—(*who did it?* I cried, *I'll tear him apart!*)—and he combs his hair every night before sleeping so he'll look good in his dreams. His coat was the colour of a young deer, but his coat is dead. His skin has a faint olive cast, and you can see the muscles working beneath it like swimmers under water. His eyes change colour according to what they are looking at. His own blood is a potent drug that lifts him to heaven or drops him into Hell; he sees colours that smell like sage and seaweed, taste like wild honey and bacon rind, sound like all the bells of the world ringing together.

He dances around telephone poles, pillars, anything that can create a centre, and his shoes go Click Click Click because there are cleats at the heel and toe. The telephone pole or pillar is trapped in the centre of his dance; he claps his hands, looks over his left shoulder and sneers at his feet. The sneer hardens into a kind of Flamenco mask, the expression of all true dancers, because their own bodies offend them.

Perhaps you have caught glimpses of the dark invisible dancer under the Bloor-Street viaduct or in such unlikely places as the Eglington subway station, Grenadier pond and so forth. If you watch closely you will realize you've seen him many times before in the black streets beneath the billboards. To you who have no need of Fairy Tales, I offer this fiction (and nothing is fiction). He walks with the studied step of a dancer who may at any moment, without warning, dance.

You may say that thousands of people in Kanada wear trench-coats with the colour of young deer. What will you do, then?—ask all the trench-coats if they are wearing *him*?

One night in his apartment—(which reminds me to mention he had a lot of money, hence could amuse himself demolishing banks once in a while—I found myself caressing a little Canaanite goddess with a pebble in her navel. I sank back with it into the forest of a dark green couch.

'Noman,' I asked, 'why don't you talk about your past?'

Then he did a strange thing. He grabbed the fat little goddess and smashed her with one stroke against the wall.

'Which part of my past do you want?' he asked. 'An arm, a leg, a tooth, a testicle?'

I hated to see him throw himself away like that. He drew back and gazed at me with his huge insolent eyes, and I told him he was a fiend. Rarely did I hand out such compliments.

'You've got me all wrong, Kali,' he said, retrieving the goddess' navel from the floor and turning it over and over in his fingers.

Then we went out and drank wine on the balcony and listened to the sweet machines and the sensual wheels of the city and got drunk on the roof of the world.

When I left, late that same night, he came down with me to the lobby of the apartment building, and I noticed the mirrors were arranged in such a way that you could see yourself reflected a million times smaller and smaller into a microcosm.

'Look,' I told him. 'I can see a thousand of you! A thousand million Nomans getting smaller and smaller!'

'I know,' he said, without turning his head.

'How do you know? You're not even looking!'

'I don't have to. I know they're all there, millions of me, travelling into infinity. I don't like infinity much, so I don't look.'

'What if all the different Nomans starting talking to each other,' I said. 'What a babble of tongues!'

'They *are* all talking to each other,' he said, and as he spoke, a thousand mouths opened and closed.

'But they're all saying the same thing! Don't any of them know different languages?'

'No,' he said. But in the mirror I saw each mouth opening and closing on a different word. *No, non, ochi, laa.* So I kissed him—partly so his mouth wouldn't speak again, partly because I wanted to see the kiss reproduced down into the microcosm. Afterwards I looked at his tongue, to see what was so foreign about it. And that night I dreamed he was the captain of an ancient ship, and all the oarsmen had his face.

I had to resist the temptation to pack suitcases for India. You can't imagine what a problem I had making both centres meet. I saw Noman as Siva in the annexes of department stores. We were dying, Egypt, dying. I screamed when noons came only at twelve o'clock. The city was sinking into quicksand. A handless glove someone left on a fence-post drove me to distraction. I had a piece of Noman's hair in my wallet, which I'd take a match to now and then, saying 'Who are you? If you don't answer I'll burn you.' And the hair would lie there, lie there smelling like a campfire in a northern forest, saying nothing.

'Noman, you're losing my mind,' I used to tell him. 'Why can't you be honest and lie once in a while? Why can't you be serious and crack a few jokes?'

I suppose what was really bothering me was the fact that my car was being fixed. I got it out of the hospital with its red upholstery all stitched up beautifully, and we went for a drive. We left the city far behind us, and I opened all the windows to let the night in. I turned up the radio to hear Moussorgsky.

'Nothing is enough, is it Kali? Nothing *suffices*.' Noman said, turning up the collar of his coat as he always did, whether to keep the world out or himself in, I never knew.

To cheer him up I said, 'The radio power output of the Cyrganus Galaxies amounts to 1,000,000,000,000,000,000,-000,000,000,000,000,000,000,000 kilowatts.'

'Kali,' he said, leaning over to me with a cigarette in his mouth, 'for heaven's sake give me a *light*!'

We turned back toward the city.

'Kali, let's spend all our money and possess ourselves! Let's possess the future as surely as we possess the past!'

'But you don't *have* a past,' I winked at him in the mirror.

'Yes I do, damn it! I'll tell you about it later. Let's become the masters of time, let's *move into* time!'

'To pave the way for our descendants?' I laughed.

'No,' he said, and looked at me strangely. 'For our *ancestors*. They're the ones who are trapped.'

I didn't feel like questioning him, so I let him go on.

'We've inherited this great Emptiness,' he said. 'An empty

door that leads into the forest and the snow. No man can get through. . . .'

'Can *you?*' I asked, though I wasn't sure what he was talking about.

'Yes,' he said, 'I think I can.'

We approached a big skyway that was under construction. It was very late and there were only a few cars passing by. He told me to park beneath one of of the huge concrete legs that were to support the overpass. For a long way the legs stretched out on either side of us. It was a kind of Stonehenge, an incomplete temple.

And then—

he stepped quickly out of the car and threw off his coat, his shirt, his socks, his shoes, and laid them in a heap at the bottom of the cold pillar. It was full moon, a November night. Then he began to dance. Around and around, in and out between the pillars, the cranes, the small trucks and pieces of machinery that had been left standing for the night. It was as if everything had been arranged for him, for his dance.

Siva, I thought, as I sat in the whirring silence of my car.

All his bones were wings; his body was like one of those beautifully designed but deadly planes they made a hundred years ago. His back, from the shoulder-blades to the bottom of his spine, was the tightly stretched, triangular frame of a kite. I imagined that the organs in his body floated in a kind of fluid tension, a suspended flight. And as he danced and flew, his body broke into alphabets!

A police car pulled up beside me then and a mouth leaned in the window of my car. 'And what, may I ask, is *he* doing?' said the mouth.

'Dancing,' I said. 'He's a dancer.'

The mouth let out a long low whistle. 'It takes all kinds,'

it said. 'I'll have to ask you both to move on. People don't dance half naked in the streets of Trawnah.'

'We're from out of town,' I said.

'No reason to dance half naked in the streets of Trawnah. What is he anyway, some kind of forriner?'

'Yes,' I said. 'Speaks a language unknown to man. A combination of Cree, Italian, Eskimo and Cabbagetown slang.'

'I wouldn't know about that,' said the mouth. 'One born every day. Dancing half naked under the overpass, beats everything. And what are *you* doing here?'

'Watching him dance half naked under the overpass,' I said.

'*Watching* him dance half naked under the overpass? Two born every day, if you ask me. Move on, lady, unless you want to tell it to the judge.'

'I am the judge,' I said, wishing I had windshield wipers on the *side* windows of the car to wipe away the mouth.

We finally left, and Noman was laughing and laughing all the way home. He had turned into a kind of vapour, a mist that I could have sprayed on my hair. When we parked outside his apartment he grabbed the gearshift and wrenched it out of position. The thing gave a sickening crunch and hung limply to one side.

I said, 'You've castrated my car.'

'Exactly,' he said, taking my arm. 'We're not going anywhere for quite a while. Come on!'

Before we went inside I saw two young lovers. They looked so frail and vulnerable; they made you feel as if you wanted to carry them across the street, call a cab, feed them. They could have been so easily run over. They were prone to all the hazards of the world. They should have carried white canes like the blind. Noman saw them too and smiled.

Inside his apartment was a kind of Eden. We lit a big fire

and threw a million things into it. I sank into the forest-green couch and dreamed that we were in a rain forest, a primeval jungle chewing green dinosaur steaks. Pterodactyls screeched anathemas overhead and we sauntered over to the Tree and lazily bit into two apples. ... The jungle went dead quiet and the Voice told us we had transgressed the first law: Thou Shalt Not Have Knowledge. 'Are you *serious?*' Noman cried. The sun stood still and the jungle turned a bright alizeran. Thunder and lightning. The odd comet. We pelted heaven with our apple cores; great dinosaurs trumpeted and fell, blinded, at our feet. Noman was livid. Then somehow Eden changed into Algonquin Park and we lay back in the dense green undergrowth and became joyfully knowledgeable.

When I awoke he was lying beside me and as I watched him I remembered something I'd heard or read or thought long before. *When you love him, pretend he can't see, only feel; pretend he is blind.* So I bit his shoulder and my teeth made the sign of the holy Fish. Then I made a trail of those *ichthys* all down his flesh like a stream of small salmon, a series of hieroglyphs or secret signs pointing the way to some forbidden rendezvous in the catacombs. Later I made other marks, strange shapeless things that made his body look like a winter landscape over which some legendary medieval beast had trodden. We dove into each other, each speaking his own separate savage tongue. When I kissed him I whispered, *This* is for the blind who love with their mouths and hands, *this* is for the children in the alleyways of the world, *this* is for all the lovers who never made it, *this*. ...

And our limbs, changing, moving, wrote out new alphabets in the darkness, formed new constellations. We smelled of salt, and fire and flowers.

Next morning I watched the sun rise over his shoulder; the light slowly probed the apartment, probed the little statues, their hands, their eyes, which had the strange stare of the blind. The floor was strewn with clothes, inner ones, outer ones. Noman's coat lay exhausted in one corner of the room. I didn't understand how my skirt was dangling from the bookshelf above the Virgil translations, nor did I have any idea how my left shoe had ended up on the tape recorder, my earrings in the ashtray, etc. The couch was strewn with fallen masks.

We emerged from the night beaten and bruised, as if we'd come out of a den of lions, or had become gladiators, bloody and victorious after the games. My loins were broken; armies had marched over them and crushed them into sand. We sat cross-legged like children proudly comparing the maps of our bodies—the birthmarks, scars, incisions, beauty-spots, all the landmarks of our lives, those we were born with and those we'd incurred. New trails broken in the forest, old signposts no longer used, footprints of forest animals who come in the night, places of fire, places of water, portages, hills.

We stayed indoors many days and I managed to get out only once—and that was just to grab supplies from the corner store for the next long siege. On Sunday morning I settled into the couch with coffee. I noticed my hair had broken out of its braids, and idly I began to re-braid it.

'Sunday,' said Noman. 'I can feel God all over the place, sneaking through the apartment, going through my desk and drawers. . . .'

I smiled and continued to tame my hair.

'Braid very slowly, Kali, and I'll tell you a long story. It's all about my Past.'

'But you don't *have*—' I protested.

'Sure I do,' he said, putting a cigarette into his mouth backwards and lighting the filter. 'I'll start anywhere. Yes, I'll start with the time I lay kissing concrete in an alleyway behind Howland Street watching the glorious army of my youth surrender to reality. Howland Street was a very rough district, and I'd been beaten up the night before. . . .'

'*Howland* Street!' I cried. 'But *everybody's* lived on Howland Street!'

'I know. Anyway, when I was eighteen I went to work in the carnival. I thought I'd find the first and last of the world's real people there in that wild crossroads of cultures. But the boss didn't want me at first, and I wandered off and saw a woman lighting a fluorescent tube with her bare hands, and I thought—what talent does that take? I told her anyone could light lamps with their fingertips, and she got mad. Her name was Futura and she passed electricity through her body eight times a day. She thought she was charged volt upon ampere with the most devastating powers. Then I saw the Valkyr, who was blonde with braids, a horned woman, ironic and strong. She was so cold she burned, like dry ice. She swallowed swords, and I thought—what talent does that take? So I wandered off again and went inside the little big tent—'

'Noman, what in hell is a *little* big tent?'

'Keep braiding and keep quiet,' he said. 'A little big tent is a circus tent that isn't very large. Inside it was empty except for a couple of guys spearing popcorn wrappers off the ground. I looked up into the silver-wired paradise at the top, the high world of the swings, and I thought of the trapeze artists, the famous flyers who never fall. I wanted to climb the ladder to where the beautiful ropes and swings hung in the silence, to float forever through the high garden of wires. To see below me the wild colours of the crowds, their faces scattered like a pile of dimes on the ground, the horses plumed like birds. I wanted to send my bones flying in all directions and be above them all, and flaunt my freedom.

'But I didn't have time to learn the craft, so I became a clown. I had great conversations with myself as I was cleaning up after the show. *I'm not a clown, I'm a genius*, I'd say to the mirror as I removed my red bulbous nose. *No-one knows I have written poetry*, I'd add, wiping off my eyebrows. *Under this absurd mask I am a holy man* (lifting off my false skull like an orange peel). *By day I'm a clown, but by night I'm the Dark and Unknown Hunter* (scraping off my mouth with a spatula). *Only I know what a façade the world is* (pulling off my costume). *When I am naked, I am more naked than most* (rolling down my stockings to my ankles. *Tell them that*, I'd say as I lathered my face.

'*Noman, you're naked*,' I'd advise the mirror.

'Well, I got sick of being a clown so I decided to acquaint myself with ropes and chains and become an escape artist. I suppose I wanted to act out some sort of allegory of freedom to feel every muscle seeking its order of performance to defeat the rope or chain, to break its central tension. I suppose I also wanted the chance to wear loud sequined leotards that drew attention to my loins. Most of the struggle came from them (I was young). I remember my first performances, when my face was a mask of pain and concentration; I remember how the Valkyr stood close by, testing her swords, weapons that could free me faster than I could free myself. The ropes were like pythons wrapped around my body. Once I twisted my hip to let one loop fall free, and all the girls giggled, because the movement had pushed part of my tights down from my waist and they were waiting to see what else would be exposed.'

'The beasts.' I said, 'The sheer beasts.'

'Keep quiet and braid,' said Noman.

'And they kept watching me, watching my private struggle, and when they felt it wasn't right to look at my legs, they looked at my arms; and when they felt they shouldn't look at my arms they looked at my face. Then they couldn't even look at my face, for I was freeing myself from the ropes, and my face must have been awful to see, and when I finally stepped out of the ropes I felt the people turn away, for I was laughing and laughing and I had no shame at all.'

I put an elastic band around the second braid, which I'd worked into place, but Noman reached out and snapped it and ruffled my hair back into chaos.

'Re-braid,' he said. 'I'm not finished.'

'Then I left the carnival and went to look for my father. . . .'

'Wait a minute! What do you mean, *look* for your father? Didn't you know where he was?'

'I wasn't even sure *who* he was. But I thought he was the one with the steel eyes, and I dreamed of going back through the fields and trees whispering, *Father, Père, Pateras, Abu, Aubrey*, through the small forest I'd known as a child and down the road where I once rode a great white horse. I thought I'd find him in the old house beside the wicked gate. The gate would give way and he would come out to greet me with ivory hair and eyebrows that flew back like the wings of small angry birds.

'And the man with no more seed in his loins would address me: *Noman. Where have you been? Sit down. Well, what? What have you been doing the last 5000 years? Tinker, tailor, soldier, sailor, beggarman, thief? Tell me, are you an athlete, a businessman, a dancer?*

'I would tell him I was Noman.'

'And he would say, *well that's food for thought. Would you like tea?* And carefully he would put on the kettle, a ritual. And I would long to see him laugh, and to see the universe break up into particles of his laughter. But he would stir the tea with his terrible hair flying back from his temples. And he would bring in the tea in a green teapot that was covered with pictures of log cabins and bears. I would hate the teapot, because he always used to love wine, and I would take the thing outside and smash it on the bricks and return, smiling. Perhaps then he would cough, dragging up the phlegm of his years, and I would start to realize he was nothing but an old man in an imaginary house, in a forest. I would see his shoes, and that would finish me. Shoes fill me with spasms of pity, always. Shoes tell tales, shoes tell the truth. Shoes are winter, and potatoes, and poverty, and snow. Achilles didn't wear shoes. Then I think I would become hysterial and cry out, *Father I think I have killed you*! And he would say, *Of course you have, my son. What else is on your mind*? And then I would be so overcome I would leave. . . .'

'Noman, for heaven's sake, these are all the things that *would* have happened. What *did* happen, did you find him?'

'Oh no,' he said. 'I just thought about it a while. Then I forgot, and became a dancer.'

My braids were by now braided so tightly they stuck out stiff from both sides of my head like cacti. The room was bright white with Sunday. We saw that we were naked and our nakedness was still full of mysteries, like the snow. . . . It was getting close to winter, and in my mind I catalogued all I knew of winter; tangerines, red scarves, Russian hats, tinkling bells, foxes.

We entered into another long siege.

When we arose the following Sunday I said, 'Noman, I have the answer to all your problems.'

'And what is it, Kali?'

'You must die.'

'That's the answer to everybody's problem,' he said.

'No,' I told him, 'I mean you must stage a mock death, a brilliant scene in which we'll all participate. Then you can be born again, maybe even assume a real name.'

He agreed and I was so happy I gave him six presents:

A desk blotter with ten multi-coloured refills.

A red bathrobe.

A sealing-wax set complete with seal.
A zodiac wallet. (He was an Aquarian.)
A record I can't remember.
A dictionary.

And so the Saturnal was staged. Down in the ravine every-thing was quiet save for the distant hum of traffic and the sound of my own voice as I recited from Poe. Noman lit a cigarette and dropped dead just as we'd planned, and blood flowed freely from the little capsules of dye concealed in his trench-coat. It snowed too, just as we'd planned, and the drama was complete.

One week later we returned to the scene of the crime, and stood on the bridge over the ravine, looking down into the little clearing where he had died. It was windy and cold. Noman smiled—(how wide his mouth was when he smiled!) —and he took the trench-coat off and threw it down into the ravine. It floated down like a great terrible bird and settled on the frozen floor of the valley.

In puris naturalibus, he said.

Next spring before Easter we drove to Ottawa and took ridiculous photos of ourselves caressing the big stone lion on Parliament Hill. Then Noman wanted to go to Kings-mere and see Mackenzie King's synthetic ruins—the walls and arches constructed out of bits of historic stone.

'I've read all about the place,' he told me. 'And I've always longed to go. It's haunted though—do you mind?'

We drove up into the Gatineau hills by night, and the black trees along the way glistened like plastic in the rain. How well the forest concealed its history!

We pulled into the parking lot at Kingsmere and Noman led me over to a small field hemmed in by trees and tiny pillars and arches, all covered with a thin film of mist and rain.

'I don't like this place,' I said, and shivered. 'It's Noman's land.'

But he laughed, and led me over the black grass toward a terrace bordered by Grecian columns.

He spotted an arch at one end of the terrace, like an ancient door that led into the forest, the final mystery.

'Do you dare to go?' he breathed. 'Are you coming, Kali?' he said, and started across the field.

I plunked myself down on the wet grass and refused to budge.

'Coming Kali?' he asked again, and when I didn't answer he went on farther into the spooky greyness nearer and nearer the arch. I half rose to follow him, but just then a sudden flash of lightning lit up the field and froze the terrible door in violent relief.

'Noman, what are we *doing* here?' I cried. 'Whose past have we stolen? Into whose future are we moving?'

And he (swiftly removing his clothes) called back to me —'Why, our own, of course!'

And blithely stepped, stark naked, through the arch.

"House of the Whale" first appeared in *Fourteen Stories
High* (Oberon), "The Second Coming of Julian the
Magician" in *Prism*, "Kingsmere" and "Day of Twelve
Princes" in *Tamarack*. "House of the Whale" has also been
broadcast on CBC *Anthology*, as have "Snow" and "The
Oarsman and the Seamstress." Several of the stories have
been revised since their first publication. Preparation of the
manuscript was made possible by a grant from the Canada
Council
Library of Congress Catalogue Card No. 72-77037
ISBN 0 88750 059 5 (hardcover)
ISBN 0 88750 060 9 (softcover)
Cover photograph by J. M. Reynolds. Book design by
Michael Macklem
Printed in England by Hazell Watson & Viney Ltd.
PUBLISHED IN CANADA BY OBERON PRESS